Divinity and Humanity

The doctrine of the Incarnation lies at the heart of Christianity. But the idea that 'God was in Christ' has become a much-debated topic in modern theology. Oliver Crisp addresses six key issues in the Incarnation, defending a robust version of the doctrine, in keeping with classical Christology. He explores perichoresis, or interpenetration, with reference to both the Incarnation and the Trinity. Over two chapters Crisp deals with the human nature of Christ and then provides an argument against the view, common among some contemporary theologians, that Christ had a fallen human nature. He considers the notion of divine kenosis or self-emptying, and discusses non-incarnational Christology, focusing on the work of John Hick. This view denies that Christ is God Incarnate, regarding him as primarily a moral exemplar to be imitated. Crisp rejects this alternative account of the nature of Christology.

OLIVER D. CRISP is Lecturer in Theology at the University of Bristol. He is author of *Jonathan Edwards and the Metaphysics of Sin* (2005).

CURRENT ISSUES IN THEOLOGY

General Editor:
Iain Torrance
President and Professor of Patristics, Princeton Theological Seminary

Editorial Advisory Board:

David Ford   *University of Cambridge*
Bryan Spinks   *Yale University*
Kathryn Tanner   *University of Chicago*
John Webster   *University of Aberdeen*

There is a need among upper-undergraduate and graduate students of theology, as well as among Christian teachers and church professionals, for a series of short, focussed studies of particular key topics in theology written by prominent theologians. *Current Issues in Theology* meets this need.

The books in the series are designed to provide a "state-of-the-art" statement on the topic in question, engaging with contemporary thinking as well as providing original insights. The aim is to publish books which stand between the static monograph genre and the more immediate statement of a journal article, by authors who are questioning existing paradigms or rethinking perspectives.

Other titles in the series:

Holy Scripture   John Webster
The Just War Revisited   Oliver O'Donovan
Bodies and Souls, or Spirited Bodies?   Nancey Murphy
Christ and Horrors   Marilyn McCord Adams

OLIVER D. CRISP

Divinity and Humanity

The Incarnation Reconsidered

CAMBRIDGE
UNIVERSITY PRESS

CAMBRIDGE UNIVERSITY PRESS
Cambridge, New York, Melbourne, Madrid, Cape Town, Singapore, São Paulo

Cambridge University Press
The Edinburgh Building, Cambridge CB2 2RU, UK

Published in the United States of America by Cambridge University Press, New York

www.cambridge.org
Information on this title: www.cambridge.org/9780521695350

First published 2007

Printed in the United Kingdom at the University Press, Cambridge

A catalogue record for this publication is available from the British Library

Library of Congress Cataloguing in Publication data
Crisp, Oliver.
Divinity and humanity: the incarnation reconsidered / Oliver D. Crisp.
    p.   cm. – (Current issues in theology ; v. 5)
Includes bibliographical references and index.
ISBN-13: 978-0-521-87352-9 (hardback)
ISBN-10: 0-521-87352-5 (hardback)
ISBN-13: 978-0-521-69535-0 (pbk.)
ISBN-10: 0-521-69535-x (pbk.)
1. Incarnation.   2. Jesus Christ–Person and offices.   3. Trinity.   I. Title.
BT220.C755   2007
232'.1–dc22
2006025227

ISBN-13 978-0-521-87352-9 hardback
ISBN-10 0-521-87352-5 hardback

ISBN-13 978-0-521-69535-0 paperback
ISBN-10 0-521-69535-x paperback

For Liberty and Elliot

Contents

Preface

This book is a small contribution to the doctrine of the person of Christ. It is physically small by comparison to a number of other books on the topic. It also covers a limited range of topics and notions pertaining to the person of Christ. There is much more to be said on this than I have been able to say here. Still, one has to begin somewhere. I have tried to tackle problems to do with the person of Christ that focus upon the relation of the divinity to the humanity of Christ. Every important issue to do with the person of Christ deals with his divinity and humanity in some fashion, even if it is only as a means to saying something else. But there are issues to do with the person of Christ that touch upon the relationship of his divinity to his humanity in particular, important ways. I have not dealt with all of them, but I have dealt with six that seemed to me to be central and defining problems in this area.

The shape of the book is as follows. There are three chapters expounding issues in a broadly Chalcedonian Christology, followed by three chapters that defend a broadly Chalcedonian Christology (as I construe it) against three doctrines that attempt to modify or, in one case, replace it.

The first chapter offers a reconsideration of the doctrine of perichoresis. This is a doctrine that has had considerable vogue in recent theology, but most of this interest has been directed towards the Trinitarian application of the doctrine (with respect to the mutual interpenetration of the different persons of the Trinity). Much less has been said about its potential for application to matters Christological. This is curious, not least because, as I argue, the application of perichoresis to Christology helps to explicate the doctrine of the union of Christ's two natures (divine and human) in important respects. The discussion in this chapter outlines a way in which Christological perichoresis might be useful, and distinguishes it from the doctrine of the communication of attributes between Christ's two natures. In a closing section, the application of perichoresis to the Trinity is also considered. The two uses of the doctrine are different, but both may be helpful in theology.

Chapters two and three deal with the human nature of Christ. In the second chapter, consideration is given to what the human nature of Christ consists in. There have been several traditional ways in which this has been understood, and, although insufficient attention has been paid to this issue in recent systematic theology, several recent philosophical discussions of the matter are helpful in surveying the terrain. I opt for a version of the medieval view of Christ's human nature: that it is a concrete particular composed of a human body and soul, assumed by the Word of God at the Incarnation. But the main alternative view, that Christ's human nature is a property of the second person of the Trinity, may also be defensible, although I do not defend it.

The third chapter builds on this discussion, considering whether or not Christ's human nature is 'impersonal', and whether it is 'person-alized', so to speak, by the Word, in his assumption of human nature. These intertwined problems, mooted in modern theology by Karl Barth among others, but with roots earlier in the tradition, are often referred to as the *anhypostatos physis* (impersonal (human) nature) and *enhypostatos physis* (personalized (human) nature), respectively. I have deliberately combined these two issues, calling their product the *en-anhypostasia* question, since the problem this raises for Christology is whether Christ's human nature is either impersonal, or personalized by the Word, or both. What this chapter shows is that an adequate answer to these issues depends on prior commitments pertaining to what Christ's human nature consists in. This is a point that has not always been appreciated in the literature.

The second section of the book, concerning revisions to a broadly Chalcedonian Christology, continues the theme of issues concerning the humanity of Christ in chapter four. There, the matter of whether or not Christ had a fallen human nature is discussed. A number of modern theologians have claimed that, in order for Christ to redeem human beings, he must assume the fallen human nature human beings possess. However, this reasoning faces considerable objections, not least the traditional notion culled from the doctrine of sin, that fallenness and moral culpability go hand in hand. I argue that the claim that Christ had a fallen human nature must be rejected, because Christ is without sin. But it is possible that Christ's human nature was affected by the Fall. After all, Christ wept, hungered, was thirsty and experienced fatigue.

Chapter five deals with another way in which a broadly Chalcedonian Christology might be revised – in this case, with respect to the notion of divine kenosis. This is, roughly, the idea that somehow the Word of God empties himself of certain divine attributes in order to become incarnate. The doctrine of divine kenosis was popular in the nineteenth and early twentieth centuries, and has become popular once more, among certain philosophical theologians. It is this recent literature that is in view in this chapter. I show that there are several strengths to divine kenosis, and that there are serious objections to the strong and the weak versions of the doctrine. However, there is a related view (which may turn out to be a weak version of the doctrine), called divine krypsis, or divine concealment. According to this view, the Word of God restricts the way in which he acts in and through his human nature, but not in any way that requires him to divest himself of his divine attributes. (This, as we shall see, takes up themes from the first chapter, on Christological perichoresis.)

The final chapter of the book concerns non-incarnational Christology. This is the view that the importance attaching to the life and work of Christ has nothing to do with a divine Incarnation, but rather with the moral example Christ puts before us as a fully but merely human being. Indeed, for many who take this view,

Christ is not God Incarnate at all. He is a mere man. This view, often associated with nineteenth-century theological liberalism, can still be found today in the work of theologians like John Hick. It is Hick's work that is the basis of discussion in this chapter, since Hick can rightly claim to be one of the clearest and most forthright defenders of a non-incarnational Christology in recent theology. I argue that there are serious shortcomings with Hick's view, the most important of which is that his doctrine cannot, in the final analysis, be considered an adequate piece of *Christian* theology, since the Incarnation is an essential constituent of Christian teaching. Removal of the Incarnation from Christology is like removal of the heart from a living human being.

Finally, let me mention two additional matters by way of introduction. First, as I have already said, my approach to Christology in this volume is 'broadly' Chalcedonian. I say this because I do not claim that my construal of Chalcedonian Christology is the only way one could make sense of the Chalcedonian definition. What is important for the arguments I lay out is that they are compatible with a Chalcedonian account of the person of Christ. I draw the reader's attention to this because I shall not do so again in the body of the text, when I refer to 'Chalcedonian Christology'.[1]

---

[1] As I shall be using the term in what follows, Chalcedonian Christology refers to that tradition in Christology which looks to the Chalcedonian definition given at the Council of Chalcedon in AD 451, for the definitive churchly pronouncement on what it is Christians should believe about the person and work of Christ, as expressed in the Scriptures, which the definition seeks to make clear. Nothing I say here suggests that this definition is a substitute for Scripture. As I understand it, the Fathers who canonized the Chalcedonian definition thought of themselves as making clear what Scripture teaches, in the face of heresies that would have undermined the teaching of Scripture in the life of the Church. I choose to deal with the Chalcedonian definition directly, rather than with Scripture, because it is a convenient summary of Christian teaching on this matter that is endorsed by the universal Church. There have been theologians in recent times who have argued that we should dispense with Chalcedonian Christology because it is confused, or somehow contrary to Scripture. For an argument against these views, see Gerald Bray, 'Can we dispense with Chalcedon?' in *Themelios* 3 (1978): 2–9.

Secondly, what is attempted here is a descriptive account of Christology, not a revisionist account. That is, this volume seeks to defend one traditional picture of the person of Christ. I am not offering a substitute for the Chalcedonian view, nor do I think one should do so. Theology should not be novel – or, at least, it should not be novel for the sake of novelty. To my mind, systematic theology should be faithful to Scripture and take seriously the chorus of voices that constitute the Christian tradition. But this means making relevant to new audiences the Gospel that has been committed to the Church. Hence, this is an essay in traditional Christology, but without being hide-bound or antique. For faithfulness to a tradition is surely consistent with new ways of thinking about that tradition, and new tools with which to make sense of its relevance for today. (Of course, new ways of thinking about a tradition are not necessarily helpful or benign. But they may be.)

Earlier versions of two chapters contained in this volume have previously appeared elsewhere:

Chapter one: 'Problems with perichoresis', in *Tyndale Bulletin* 56 (2005): 118–140;

Chapter four: 'Did Christ have a *fallen* human nature?', in *International Journal of Systematic Theology* 6 (2004): 270–288.

I am grateful to the editors and publishers of these journals for allowing this work to be reproduced here.

As with the writing of any piece of theology, this work has been considerably enhanced by the attention given to it by the following friends and colleagues: Claire Crisp, Chris Eberle, Tom Flint (whose help was invaluable for chapters two and three), Steve Guthrie, Trevor Hart, Daniel Hill, Hugh McCann, Richard Muller, Michael Pace, Robin Parry, Myron Penner, Alvin Plantinga, Luke Potter, Richard Sturch and Alan Torrance. Paul Helm and Mike Rea deserve special thanks for reading the entire manuscript in draft (in Paul Helm's case, more than once!) and offering many helpful comments that saved me from not a few errors. Tom McCall read a number of the chapters and pointed out several mistakes, particularly with respect to kenoticism. Gavin D'Costa read through the material on John Hick to my considerable benefit. Chapter one was the Tyndale House Philosophy of Religion Lecture for 2004. An earlier version of chapter four was presented at a theology seminar in St Mary's College, University of St Andrews. Much of chapter two was presented at a seminar in Calvin Theological Seminary. I am grateful to those present on these different occasions for raising issues that helped me see several matters more clearly than I had done beforehand.

I would also like to register my thanks to the Center for Philosophy of Religion, University of Notre Dame, where the bulk of this book was written during a research fellowship in the academic year 2004–2005. The faculty and staff of the Center, as well as the other fellows there, made writing this volume stimulating and enjoyable. I am doubly indebted to Iain Torrance. Not only did he encourage me to write the book for this series, but also, some years ago when I was an undergraduate, he was the first person who made me seriously think I might become a theologian. Finally, I would like to thank Kate Brett of the Cambridge University Press, who was most gracious and helpful at several points along the way.

This volume is dedicated to my children, Liberty Alice Crisp and Elliot Anselm Crisp, who ask the best theological questions that I have ever heard.

1 | Problems with perichoresis

However, the idea of perichoresis . . . quickly became a trinitarian rather than a Christological term, and the concept of a perichoresis between the two natures in the incarnate Mediator was never developed.

Donald Macleod

Perichoresis could be regarded as a kind of theological black box. It has been used in the history of theology as a means of filling a conceptual gap in reflection upon the Trinity and the hypostatic union in the Incarnation. This gap has to do with how it is that the two natures of Christ, or the persons of the Trinity, can be said to be united in such an intimate way that, in the case of the Trinity, there are 'not three gods, but one god', and, in the case of the hypostatic union, that there are not two entities in one body, but two natures held together in perfect union in one person. Perichoresis fills this gap with the notion that the two natures of Christ and the persons of the Trinity somehow interpenetrate one another, yet without confusion of substance or commingling of natures. But what does it mean to say that the persons of the Trinity exist in perichoretic unity, mutually interpenetrating one another, or that the two natures of Christ subsist perichoretically, in a hypostatic union?

This chapter is an attempt to make some sense of these two applications of the doctrine of perichoresis to the Incarnation and Trinity. Although a complete analysis of the doctrine is not possible, I think enough can be said by way of explanation to make this doctrine clear enough for the theological purposes it serves. I say that a complete analysis of perichoresis with respect to the hypostatic union, or the ontology of the Trinity, is not possible because the Trinity and Incarnation are divine mysteries. Since perichoresis is a theological concept that bears upon these two mysteries, by trying to make clear something of the ontology of the hypostatic union and the Trinity, it too touches upon things mysterious. By the term 'mystery' I mean some doctrine or notion that is beyond the ken of human beings, or beyond the limits of human reason, not a doctrine or notion that is somehow confused or contradictory. Peter van Inwagen seems to me to be correct in this regard, when, in speaking of the mysterious nature of the Trinity, he says:

> It may be that it is important for us to know that God is (somehow) three Persons in one Being and not at all important for us to have any inkling of how this could be – or even to be able to answer alleged demonstrations that it is self-contradictory. It may be that we cannot understand how God can be three Persons in one Being. It may be that an intellectual grasp of the Trinity is forever beyond us. And why not, really? It is not terribly daring to suppose that reality may contain things whose natures we cannot understand.[1]

Nevertheless, trying to understand something of what perichoresis means with application to the Incarnation and Trinity is a worthwhile enterprise, even if it is not possible to fully explain or comprehend it. If we try to pursue our reflections upon matters theological in the tradition of faith seeking understanding, then there is a right place for 'thinking God's thoughts after him', and reasoned reflection about theistic metaphysics. Part of that tradition, at least as I understand it, is that we pursue our thinking in the knowledge that we can know the mysteries of God only in faltering and partial ways. Thus theologizing and philosophizing about these matters must be

---

[1] See 'And yet there are not three Gods but one God', in Thomas V. Morris, ed., *Philosophy and The Christian Faith* (Notre Dame, IN: University of Notre Dame Press, 1988), p. 243.

tempered with humility in the face of the incomprehensibility of divine mystery.[2]

Two applications of perichoresis

In what follows we shall distinguish between two doctrines of perichoresis via the following designations: *nature-perichoresis,* denoting the perichoretic relation that exists in the hypostatic union of Christ's two natures in Incarnation, and *person-perichoresis,* denoting the perichoretic relations that exist between the persons of the Trinity.[3] These two versions of perichoresis are two generic forms of the doctrine. This is because the designation of a doctrine of perichoresis as 'nature'-perichoresis, or 'person'-perichoresis serves only to distinguish these two applications of perichoresis in theology, not to circumscribe, or express, what constitutes the substance of the doctrine in each of these two cases. There are, in fact, a number of different versions of each of nature- and person-perichoresis, as we shall see. The task of this chapter is to attempt to analyse perichoresis in order to show which versions of this doctrine are coherent and

---

[2] I should point out that what follows will not offer an *explanation* of what it means to say that the persons of the Trinity exist in perichoretic unity, mutually interpenetrating each other. While I will have something to say by way of distinguishing between perichoresis in the Trinity and in the Incarnation, the focus here is principally on the application of perichoresis to the Incarnation, not to the Trinity. My point here about the mysterious nature of perichoresis goes for its application to both the Trinity and the Incarnation.

[3] Richard Swinburne points out the Greek terms for these two doctrines in *The Christian God* (Oxford: Oxford University Press, 1993), p. 209, n. 20. They are *perichoresis physeon* and *perichoresis hypostaton* respectively. I have not followed Swinburne in this designation, though it has the *imprimatur* of patristic theology, because it seems to be rather confusing to talk about the hypostatic union of Christ and *physic perichoresis* on the one hand, and the perichoretic relations in the Trinity as *hypostatic* on the other. Besides, as Professor Alan Torrance reminded me, there are a host of theological controversies surrounding the concept of *hypostasis* and its cognates, which I am keen to avoid here.

which are not. We shall examine both of these versions of perichoresis, beginning with nature-perichoresis and the person of Christ.

The *communicatio idiomatum* and nature-perichoresis

The history of the concept of perichoresis has to do as much with misunderstandings between some of the Church Fathers about what the concept means as it has to do with reflection upon the hypostatic union and persons of the Trinity. For this reason, the historical development of the doctrine is important for understanding the conceptual development that it involved.[4] Put in barest outline, perichoresis was first used by some of the Fathers to make sense of the hypostatic union, and only later taken up as a means of explicating the ontology of the Trinity. The patristic scholar Leonard Prestige says that perichoresis was first used by Gregory Nazianzen in the fourth century AD, in his *Epistle 101* and elsewhere, and was subsequently deployed in the work of Maximus the Confessor. Both of these early Christian theologians used the concept to refer to the hypostatic union only. Thus Gregory in *Epistle 101* says, 'Just as the natures are mixed, so also the names pass reciprocally into each other by the principle of this coalescence.'[5] Randall Otto comments on this passage: 'Perichoresis thus signifies the attribution of one nature's prerogatives to the other, subsequently termed *communicatio idiomatum* [communication of attributes], by virtue of the interpenetration, but not commingling, of these [two] natures.'[6]

---

4   See, for example, Randall Otto, 'The use and abuse of Perichoresis in recent theology', *Scottish Journal of Theology* 54 (2001), pp. 366–384; G. L. Prestige, 'ΠΕΡΙΧΟΡΕω and ΠΕΡΙΧΟΡΕΣΙΣ in the Fathers', *Journal of Theological Studies* 29 (1928), pp. 242–252; Richard Cross, 'Christological predication in John of Damascus', *Mediaeval Studies* 62 (2000), pp. 69–124; and Wolfhart Pannenberg, *Jesus – God and Man*, 2nd edn, trans. Lewis L. Wilkins and Duane A. Priebe (Philadelphia: Westminster Press, 1977). My rendition of the historical material owes much to these sources.

5   Gregory, *Epistle 101*, in *Patrologia Graeca* 37.181C, cited in Otto, 'The use and abuse of perichoresis, p. 368.

6   Ibid.

In a similar fashion, according to Prestige, Maximus maintained that the human nature of Christ reciprocates with the divine nature of Christ: 'The metaphor is still that employed by Gregory: the two opposites are revealed as complementary sides of a single concrete object by the rotation of that object: the two natures reciprocate not merely in name, as with Gregory, but in practical effect and operation.'[7] It is important to note that, in this early version of nature-perichoresis, there is no clear notion of interpenetration.[8] It was John of Damascus in the mid-seventh century AD who took perichoresis and applied it to the doctrine of the Trinity in his treatise *De fide orthodoxa* ('On the orthodox faith'). In the process he introduced the notion of interpenetration into the discussion of the doctrine in a technical fashion, rather than, as with Gregory of Nazianzus, in passing. However, this introduction of the term 'interpenetration' came about, according to Prestige, via a misunderstanding of Maximus' work. The doctrine of perichoresis prior to John Damascene seems to be closer to, although perhaps not the same as, a doctrine of the *communicatio idiomatum* or communication of attributes. Thus, it appears, there was an important conceptual change in the way perichoresis was understood as the doctrine was developed.[9]

However, it is important not to confuse the communication of attributes with nature-perichoresis. The doctrine of the communication of attributes has to do with how apparently contradictory properties can be predicated of the one person of Christ, while holding the two natures together in the hypostatic union without confusing or conflating them. (For instance, the apparently contradictory

---

7 Prestige, 'ΠΕΡΙΧΟΡΕⲰ and ΠΕΡΙΧΟΡΕΣΙΣ in the Fathers', p. 243. Compare Otto, who cites Maximus as follows: 'The human nature interpenetrates the divine nature, to which it is united without any confusion.' From *Ambiguorum Liber* 112b, *Patrologia Graeca* 91.1053, in Otto, 'The use and abuse of Perichoresis', p. 369.

8 A point noted by Pannenberg. He comments, 'The Cappadocians in the fourth century still conceive this unity rather carelessly as a mixture.' *Jesus – God and Man*, p. 297.

9 See Cross's article 'Christological predication in John of Damascus' for a more nuanced account of this.

properties of 'being created at a particular time' and 'being eternal', which seem to be in the background of Christ's declaration, in John 8.58: 'Before Abraham was born, I am.') The doctrine of nature-perichoresis has to do with how the two natures are united in the hypostatic union. It does not give a complete explanation of how the two natures are united, but it goes some way to showing how they might be united together. In particular, in those versions of nature-perichoresis after John of Damascus, it has to do with how the two natures of Christ can be said to interpenetrate one another without confusing or commingling of the natures, and without generating a *tertium quid* (that is, a third sort of thing made up of the fusion of the two natures, or parts of the two natures thereof). To make clear just how it is that the communication of attributes is not the same as nature-perichoresis (Gregory and Maximus notwithstanding), we shall consider each of these two doctrines in turn.[10]

The communicatio idiomatum

There are several ways in which the doctrine of the *communicatio idiomatum* could be construed. The weakest form of the communication of attributes involves no transference of properties from one of the natures of Christ to the other. Instead, the properties of the divine nature and the properties of the human nature are both predicated of the person of Christ. In this way the integrity of both natures is preserved, without the confusion or commingling of either. It is also the case, according to this version of the doctrine, that things belonging to one nature alone cannot be predicated of the other nature in

---

[10] Donald Macleod says that nature-perichoresis was never taken up by the Church (see the superscription at the beginning of this chapter). Instead, the communication of attributes was thought sufficient to the purpose of making sense of the hypostatic union. On the view I shall develop, one could hold both doctrines according to an orthodox (that is, biblical and Chalcedonian) Christology. See Macleod, *The Person of Christ* (Leicester: Inter-Varsity Press, 1998), p. 194.

the communication of attributes. This means that it is true to say that Christ is both omnipotent and yet unable to perform miracles at Nazareth because of the lack of faith among the villagers, and that he is all-knowing and yet ignorant of the time of his second coming, and so forth. But it would be false, on this understanding of the communication of attributes, to say things like 'Christ is ignorant in his divinity', or 'Christ is omnipotent in his humanity.'[11] This notion can be found in Pope Leo's *Tome*:

> Since then the properties of both natures and substances were preserved and co-existed in One Person, humility was embraced by majesty, weakness by strength, mortality by eternity; and to pay the debt of our condition the inviolable nature was united to a passible nature; so that, as was necessary for our healing, there was one and the same 'Mediator between God and men, the man Jesus Christ,' who was capable of death in one nature and incapable of it in the other. In the complete and perfect nature, therefore, of every man, very God was born – complete in what belonged to Him, complete in what belonged to us.[12]

We could express this weak version of the communication of attributes in the following way:

Weak *communicatio idiomatum*: The attribution of the properties of each of the natures of Christ to the person of Christ, such that the theanthropic *person* of Christ is treated as having divine and human attributes at one and the same time, yet without predicating attributes of one nature that properly belong to the other nature in the hypostatic union, without transference of properties between the

---

[11] See Ludwig Ott, *Fundamentals of Catholic Dogma* (Rockford, IL: Tan Books, 1960), bk III, pt 1, § 1, ch. 5, § 21, p. 161.

[12] T. H. Bindley, *The Ecumenical Documents of the Faith*, 4th edn (Westport, CN: Greenwood Press, 1950), p. 226.

natures and without confusing or commingling the two natures of Christ or the generation of a *tertium quid*.[13]

However, it seems paradoxical to suggest that both divine and human properties can be predicated of the person of Christ. If we were to say merely that Christ is omnipotent and limited in power without qualification, this would, indeed, appear paradoxical, if not contradictory. However, we could say that the person of Christ is said to be omnipotent and limited in power with the qualifications 'according to his divine nature' and 'according to his human nature' respectively. In this case the person of Christ may be said to be both omnipotent and physically limited in power, provided it is borne in mind that each of these statements refers, strictly speaking, to the particular nature that each property belongs to (omnipotence to the divine nature; physical limitation to the human nature), held in the hypostatic union of the person of Christ.[14] In this way, some sense can be made of reference to the person of Christ in terms of properties that belong to both his human and his divine nature.

But there is a stronger way in which the communication of attributes could be understood. This stronger sense incorporates the central insight of the weaker view, which is that the properties of both natures can be attributed to the person of Christ. But, in addition to

---

13 The use of the phrase 'theanthropic person of Christ' (that is, the God-Mannish person of Christ) guards against claiming that Christ is a human person, which seems rather odd at first glance. But I take it that a constituent of Chalcedonian Christology is that Christ is a divine person possessing a human nature, not both a divine and a human person, or merely a human person, both of which would be theologically unorthodox. In what follows, where Christ is spoken of as a person, the reader should understand this to mean 'theanthropic person of Christ'.

14 From this it follows that if Jesus is ignorant *qua* human, then the inference from 'x is F according to x's K nature' to 'x is F' is invalid. But then, it is not the person of Christ who is ignorant, but his divine nature. This raises the following question: What work is the reduplication doing when applied to the person of Christ (i.e. Christ is ignorant *qua* human, not *qua* divine)? All it does is make clear that in predicating certain things of Christ, we must be aware that there is a certain group of attributes which pertain to one nature alone, not to the whole person of Christ.

this, it also maintains that there is a real transference of properties between the two natures of Christ. This view is traditionally associated with Lutheran theology.[15] So, for example, in his developed views on the matter Luther says: 'The two natures dwell in the Lord Christ, and yet He is but one person. These two natures retain their properties, and each also communicates its properties to the other.'[16] One way of construing this is to say that there is a real transfer of (some) properties from the divine to the human nature, and vice versa. This seems to be the view of Luther in some of his later works.[17] Then, the divine nature would possess properties of the human nature, and the human nature would possess properties of the divine nature, because each nature shares its properties in common in the hypostatic union, yet without confusion of the two natures.[18] But, without important qualifications, this appears to be false. For I take it that no two natures can share all and only the same properties as each other, and remain distinct entities. That is, if two things share all the same properties and only the same properties, having no properties that they do not hold in common, then they are the same thing.

---

[15] Although the issues discussed in the Reformation debate about the communication of attributes were part of a much older controversy, between the rival schools of Christology in the patristic period. Pannenberg makes this clear in *Jesus – God and Man*, p. 298.

[16] *Luther's Works*, XXII, pp. 491–492, cited in Dennis Ngien, 'Chalcedonian Christology and beyond: Luther's understanding of the communicatio idiomatum', *Heythrop Journal* 45 (2004), p. 59. Ngien prefaces this citation with the following: 'Did Luther go beyond the traditional view, conceiving in the person of Christ the idea of a real communication of attributes between the two natures themselves? The answer is yes.'

[17] See Ngien, 'Chalcedonian Christology and beyond'. See also Louis Berkhof, *Systematic Theology* (Edinburgh: Banner of Truth, 1988 [1939]), pp. 325–326. For a standard (conservative) Lutheran account of the communication of attributes, see Francis Pieper, *Christian Dogmatics*, II (St Louis, MO: Concordia Publishing House, 1951), pp. 129ff.

[18] This sort of view makes more sense if the natures of Christ are understood to be sets of properties, rather than, as I shall be using the term, concrete particulars. I shall explain this distinction in chapter two.

To make this clear, consider the following. Let an individual essence denote a set of properties, which, held by a particular property-bearer – a substance – individuates that particular thing.[19] Now, if the two natures of Christ share all and only the same properties as each other, then they have the same essence. This is the case where a version of the principle of the identity of indiscernibles applies. If a particular nature, *a*, has a certain set of properties *F*, and another nature, *b*, has a certain set of properties *G*, and all the properties *F* of *a* are the same as all the properties *G* of *b*, and neither nature has properties that are not shared between the sets of properties *F* and *G*, then it would seem that there is nothing to distinguish *a* from *b*: they are identical.[20] But this cannot be the case with regard to the hypostatic union, precisely because it is a union between two distinct natures in one person, not merely a single nature, nor one nature under two different names, nor the fusion of two natures together

---

[19] An individual essence is to be distinguished from a kind essence. A kind essence comprises all those properties essential to a particular thing belonging to a particular kind, such as the kind 'horse' to which the thing called 'Champion the Wonder Horse' belongs. Christ has an individual essence, but this could comprise two kind essences, one human and one divine, if, and only if, all substances have *at most* one individual essence and all substances have *at least* one kind essence. In which case, Christ has his human essence contingently, but his divine essence essentially. I should point out that kind and individual essences should not be confused with natures, although in the current literature they are often used as synonyms. A nature might be a concrete particular – a substance of some sort. This is how I understand the term 'human nature'. An essence is not a substance, it is just a set of properties. Thomas Morris has defended a view similar to this in the recent literature. See *The Logic of God Incarnate* (Ithaca: Cornell University Press, 1986), chs. 2–3.

[20] There are well-known problems with some versions of the identity of indiscernibles, for instance, the idea that there could be a possible world containing only two qualitatively identical brass spheres placed at a certain distance from each other. In such a world it looks as if both objects have all the same properties including the same relational properties, but are distinct objects. But it would be very odd to think that this sort of counter-example applies to the two natures of Christ. Credally orthodox theology seems to require more than the fact that each of Christ's two natures is self-identical to distinguish between them! For one thing, the divine nature of Christ has certain properties essentially that the human nature does not, such as 'necessarily being a member of the divine Trinity'.

into one. So if Luther means to suggest that all the properties of the two natures of Christ are shared together via some transference of properties in the hypostatic union, and there are no properties that one or other nature shares that are not held in common via the hypostatic union, then the two natures are, in fact, fused into a third nature in the hypostatic union.[21]

There is a related problem that we need to clear up before further consideration of the matter of properties being transferred between Christ's two natures. Alvin Plantinga, in the course of a discussion on the essential properties of objects in his book *The Nature of Necessity*, enunciates the following principle: *Any property P had essentially by anything is had essentially by everything that has it.*[22] Is this principle true? If it is, then it would appear to pose a considerable problem for any talk of the communication of attributes, or even nature-perichoresis. For suppose God has all his attributes essentially. That is, God cannot cease to have any of the properties or predicates without ceasing to be God (a traditional theological claim). On Plantinga's principle, if the divine nature of the Word has these divine properties, and some or all of them are transferred to the human nature of Christ, this means that the human nature of Christ has these divine properties essentially. But what would it mean to say that a human being is essentially omnipresent, or essentially omnipotent – or, worse still, has all the properties of a divine person *essentially*? I suggest that this would be very strange indeed. In fact, if it is essential to human beings that they are, say, spatially limited in some sense, then it cannot be the case that Christ's human nature is essentially omnipresent.

It seems to me that there is no problem in thinking that a particular object may have certain essential properties that, through some

---

[21] My use of the notion of transference of properties should be distinguished from the so-called communicable attributes of God. God is said in classical theology to have certain attributes that may be communicated to his creatures, e.g. 'Be holy, for I am holy.' But this is not what is in view here.

[22] See Alvin Plantinga, *The Nature of Necessity* (Oxford: Oxford University Press, 1974), p. 68.

process of transference, or, perhaps, divine imputation (whereby God treats one object as if it were a second object for certain theological purposes – the most obvious one being the doctrine of the imputation of sin), God transfers/imputes to another object. And I do not see why, in the case of Christ, this need involve the transferred or imputed properties being essential to the object (Christ's human nature) to which they are transferred or imputed. That is, Christ's divine nature may be essentially omniscient, and Christ's human nature only contingently omniscient, according to some notion of the communication of attributes. And, as Plantinga points out, there are numerous counter-examples to his principle, such as the properties 'being Socrates or Greek', or 'being black or white'. It is not a necessary truth that all things that have either of these properties have them essentially, although there are objects that do have them essentially, like Socrates the Greek philosopher, or a white billiard ball. So it is not necessarily the case that just because Christ's divine nature has a property essentially, if that property is transferred or imputed to his human nature, this means that his human nature has this property essentially too. There may be reasons why God restricts this property-transference to Christ, reasons to do with the hypostatic union (e.g. Christ alone of all human beings is a divine person with a human nature). And there may also be reasons why Christ exhibits certain divine attributes *qua* human only after his glorification (a matter to which we shall return). But, provided the property transference involved in the hypostatic union does not require that an essential property of the divine nature become an essential property of the human nature of Christ – and I see no reason to think this does occur – Plantinga's principle need not be an obstacle to our discussion of the communication of attributes, or of nature-perichoresis.

To return to the point about what Luther believed regarding property transference in the Incarnation, defenders of a strong version of the communication of attributes need not believe that Christ has all the divine attributes as a human being, or that he has these attributes essentially. Luther himself was not consistent on this matter, and probably in any case some of what he says in this regard should be taken as rhetorical flourish or hyperbole, rather than sober metaphysics. But even if a defender of the strong view of the communication of attributes were to claim only that the two natures of Christ (somehow) share many but not all of their properties in the hypostatic union via the transfer of certain properties (had contingently by his human nature), and that this is what the communication of attributes means, this seems false. For this would entail that, among other things, the divine nature is simultaneously omnipresent and physically limited, and omnipotent but limited in power, and so on. And it would mean that the human nature was simultaneously limited in power but also omnipotent, and physically limited but also omnipresent, which is obviously nonsense.[23]

It could be that only two properties are shared in the hypostatic union between the two natures, one from each of the two natures, and that each of these two properties denotes a different sort of power or ability, which the nature from whom the property is transferred possesses. This would be the case where omnipresence via the divine nature, and limited power via the human nature, were the only two properties shared in the hypostatic union. But although it does not seem, *prima facie*, to be metaphysically impossible for one being to have both these properties simultaneously, it is, I take it, metaphysically impossible for the human nature of Christ and the divine nature of Christ to possess both properties individually and together at one and the same time. For then each of the two natures would be powerless and omnipotent simultaneously and individually (even if they do not have both properties essentially). But the divine nature

---

[23] Could it not be said in defence of Lutherans that, once glorified, Christ's body possesses omnipresence and that this supplants the physical limitation of his pre-glorification human body? I cannot see how. Claiming that a human body could be corporeally located in every place, or co-located with every physical particle in every place, seems rather like saying that a steel bar could be composed of a stable liquid at room temperature, or a piece of wood could have the same atomic number as gold.

cannot be both omnipresent and powerless without ceasing to be divine, because this entails that the divine nature is both omnipotent and limited in power, which is contradictory. But neither can a human nature have both of these properties at one and the same time, because a human nature cannot be omnipresent and limited to a particular physical location. Yet this is what this construal of the strong version of communication of attributes requires. So it, too, is false.

Some Lutheran scholastic theologians have taken the view that the transfer of properties according to the strong version of the communication of attributes is unidirectional, from the divine to the human nature, and not vice versa.[24] This would mean that the human nature has properties in common with the divine nature in virtue of the transference of properties in the hypostatic union, but that the converse is not the case. But as it stands such a conception of strong communication of attributes is ambiguous. It could mean that *all* the divine attributes are transferred to the human nature of Christ in the hypostatic union, but not vice versa. In which case, this is problematic for reasons similar to those in the version of the Lutheran account where there is a transfer of one or more properties between both natures. It would be very peculiar to think that a human nature can remain a human nature if it has *all* the properties of the divine nature. (It also does not seem to make sense to claim that the divine attributes are communicated to the human nature of Christ in a unidirectional fashion. If the human nature of Christ is omnipresent, then presumably everything has the properties of his human nature, including every created thing, and every divine thing – but this is monumentally counter-intuitive.[25])

---

[24] The so-called *genus maiestaticum* of Lutheran Christology. See Pieper, *Christian Dogmatics*, II, pp. 152ff.

[25] Perhaps a Lutheran theologian could counter this particular point by rephrasing the *genus maiestaticum*. If it is claimed merely that the transfer of properties originates with the divine nature, then this would appear to make more sense, but it still has the counter-intuitive consequences already stated.

Alternatively, this conception of the communication of attributes could mean that some but not all of the divine attributes are transferred from the divine to the human nature in the hypostatic union, but not vice versa. Some theologians, perhaps seeing the problems inherent in such ambiguity, have opted for this more parsimonious claim. In scholastic theology, this is often done by dividing the divine attributes into two groups. The first group comprises the so-called *operative attributes* of God, such as omnipotence, omnipresence and omniscience; the second group, the so-called *quiescent attributes*, such as infinity and eternity. It is the operative, not quiescent, attributes that are transferred in this way. Then, on this version of the doctrine, the human nature has only *certain* properties in common with the divine nature in virtue of the transference of properties in the hypostatic union, but the converse is not the case, and there is no confusion of the two natures. This version of the strong doctrine of the communication of attributes appears the most promising. It requires only that one or more, but not all, of the properties of the divine nature are transferred to the human nature.

I am inclined to think that something like this does obtain in the case of the *glorified* human nature of Christ, but not in the case of his (or any other) non-glorified human nature. If that is so, this version of the strong doctrine of the communication of attributes – call it the moderate version – does make sense of Christ's human nature provided it is in a certain state, the state of glorification post-resurrection. One reason for thinking this is that it is notoriously difficult to state what the necessary and sufficient conditions for being human are. It might be metaphysically possible, for all we know, for a human being to be omnipotent and omniscient. However, I do not think it is metaphysically possible for a human being to be omnipresent, either before or after glorification. This is important because some Lutheran orthodox theologians of the post-Reformation period used this moderate version of the communication of attributes to provide the metaphysical underpinning for their sacramental teaching about the real, and ubiquitous, corporeality of Christ's body, developed in the doctrine of consubstantiation.[26] To show why the transfer of this particular property from the divine to the human nature is untenable, consider the following reasoning.

First, assume that omnipresence, an essential property of the divine nature, is transferred to the human nature in the hypostatic union. It follows that, after this property has been transferred from the divine to the human nature of Christ, the human nature of Christ is omnipresent. That is, from the moment of hypostatic union onward, in all subsequent moments of the existence of Christ, the human nature of Christ is omnipresent.[27] (If this property-transfer takes place at the moment of hypostatic union, then, this would seem to be at the moment of the virginal conception of Christ. In which

---

[26] This is a version of a real-presence doctrine of the Eucharist. That is, Lutheran sacramental theology states that Christ is really, physically present in the elements of bread and wine at the mass. The formula used by Lutheran theologians is that the body of Christ is *corporeally present in, with and under* the elements. Hence, consubstantiation. This doctrine was a source of considerable conflict with the Reformed scholastic theologians. Lutheran theologians applied to the strong version of communication of attributes in order to establish that Christ can be corporeally present in the elements because his body is ubiquitous. (It is ubiquitous because this property is transferred from the divine nature to the human nature of Christ in the hypostatic union.) Lutherans like Francis Pieper dislike the term 'ubiquitous', preferring to speak of the repletive or supernatural mode of subsistence of Christ's human nature. See Pieper, *Christian Dogmatics*, II (St Louis: Concordia, 1951), pp. 180–181.

[27] What if we say that omnipresence is just something like being able to bring about any change in the universe immediately, without any intermediary, as Richard Swinburne seems to construe this? Well, this may well apply to the divine nature of Christ, but not to his human nature. Even if it applies to the human nature of Christ such that he is able to bring about any change in the universe immediately through his human soul, this is not the same as the claim I am making here (compatible with Lutheran sacramental teaching) that Christ is *corporeally* present everywhere, or co-located with every particle at every place. Such an omnipresent corporeality is, it seems to me, too metaphysically exotic to be plausible. See Swinburne, *The Coherence of Theism*, rev. edn (Oxford: Oxford University Press, 1993), ch. 7.

case, there is no prior time at which the human nature of Christ exists without the property of omnipresence, even if there is a logically prior 'moment' at which the human nature of Christ exists without this property. Of course, and in keeping with what has just been said, it could take place at Christ's glorification instead. In which case, the relevant changes to the precise moment of transfer would need to be made in the reasoning that follows.) Assume that omnipresence is a property essential to the divine nature, and that the transfer of this property means that the property becomes an essential property in the nature to which it is transferred. Then, at all temporal moments after the hypostatic union, the human nature of Christ is essentially omnipresent.[28] But this is obviously false. For then, at every moment after the hypostatic union, Christ's humanity would exist everywhere (a view the Lutherans embraced in their doctrine of the repletive or supernatural presence of Christ in the elements of the sacrament – and everywhere else[29]). But it seems to me obviously false that my hand, or the cup of tea I had this morning, or the trees outside this building, are interpenetrated in every particle by, or co-located with, Christ's *human* nature. Even if I were disposed to reject the notion that an essential property of human beings is that any human is located in a particular space at a particular time, so that I could claim that Christ's omnipresent flesh is a strange but not necessarily metaphysically impossible sort of physicality, this would still have consequences so monumentally counter-intuitive that the

---

[28] But, perhaps this property-transfer means that omnipresence is only an accidental property of Christ's human nature. Even if this is so, provided Christ's human nature retains this property at all moments subsequent to its transfer, the same objection applies.

[29] Compare Pieper's characterization of this property of Christ (citing Luther): 'A thing is at places repletively, or supernaturally, that is, when something is simultaneously and entirely in all places and fills all places, and is still gauged by no place, or encompassed by no place, where it is.' *Christian Dogmatics*, II, pp. 181, from Luther, St Louis edn, xx, pp. 949, 951. To which Pieper adds: 'Whoever believes the fact that the human nature [of Christ] was assumed into the Person of the Son of God . . . is no longer entitled to deny the omnipresence of Christ's human nature.' Ibid.

doctrine would seem to be absurd. Yet this seems to be the obvious consequence of this position.

However, it is not obviously absurd to claim Christ's human nature, once glorified, is omnipotent and omniscient. There are biblical grounds for thinking that, prior to his resurrection, Christ does not have these properties *qua* human (e.g. Matt. 24.36 and Mark 6.5). It may be that an unglorified human nature may not have these properties but a glorified human nature can. If so, this does not appear to be a matter of what is metaphysically possible, but what God has ordained is the case. And perhaps this is an instance of the medieval distinction between the absolute power of God (*de potentia absoluta*) and the ordained power of God (*de potentia ordinata*).[30] The absolute power of God is, roughly, what it is metaphysically possible for God to bring about, and the ordained power is what God has decreed will be the case. Then, it might be metaphysically possible for God to give all human natures certain properties that they do not have in the actual world, including omnipotence and omniscience. But God has ordained that this is not how things actually are. In any case, it seems to me that, though there appears to be no metaphysical impossibility about the limited transfer of some properties from the divine to the human nature of Christ in the hypostatic union, such a transfer does not occur in human natures that are not glorified, and perhaps even then only in the case of Christ's human nature once glorified. Thus, it seems plausible to suppose that a weak version of the communication of attributes may apply in the case of human natures, Christ's included, prior to glorification. But perhaps a stronger version of the communication of attributes applies to Christ's glorified human nature (provided this does not include the idea that he is corporeally omnipresent post-resurrection, as the Lutherans maintain).

[30] For an interesting recent discussion of this medieval distinction, see Paul Helm, *John Calvin's Ideas* (Oxford: Oxford University Press, 2004), ch. 11.

Nature-perichoresis

As we have already seen, the communication of attributes, in either its weak or or its strong form, is sometimes conflated with nature-perichoresis. This is a mistake. The two notions, though related, are distinct. I take it that nature-perichoresis involves an asymmetrical relation between the two natures of Christ. The divine nature of Christ penetrates his human nature without confusion and without being mingled with it. But the human nature of Christ does not penetrate the divine nature in any way. This need not be arbitrary. This asymmetry is in part due to the fact that the divine nature exists prior to the Incarnation, whereas the (individualized) human nature does not. Moreover, this penetration of the human nature by the divine nature of Christ does not involve the transfer of properties from the divine to the human nature.[31] The two natures remain distinct, but united, rather as the oxygen and haemoglobin in oxygenated red blood cells in the human body are chemically distinct, but fused together to make oxyhaemoglobin in order to deliver oxygen to the body efficiently.

This nature-perichoresis could be understood as a special case of the divine interpenetration of the created order on certain views of divine providence. Just as the divine nature might be said to interpenetrate the whole of creation, sustaining it and upholding it at each moment of its continued existence, so also the divine nature of Christ interpenetrates the human nature of Christ, upholding and sustaining it at each moment of its existence. This would seem to mean that the difference between these two instances of divine interpenetration is one of degree rather than of kind.[32]

---

[31] In here and what follows, defenders of divine simplicity should substitute 'predicates' for 'properties'.

[32] Compare Thomas: 'Although the Word of God by His power penetrates all things, conserving all, that is, and supporting all, it is to the intellectual creatures, who can properly enjoy the Word and share with Him, that from a kind of kinship of likeness He can be both more eminently and more ineffably united.' *Summa contra Gentiles* IV.41.13.

John Damascene is credited with developing a notion of nature-perichoresis like this one in his treatise *De fide orthodoxa*. He also seems to advocate a weak version of the communication of attributes (but that need not detain us here).[33] Of nature-perichoresis he says:

> But observe that although we hold that the natures of the Lord permeate one another, yet we know that the permeation springs from the divine nature. For it is that that penetrates and permeates all things, as it wills, while nothing penetrates it: and it is it, too, that imparts to the flesh its own peculiar glories, while abiding itself impassible and without participation in the affections of the flesh.
>
> (*De fide orthodoxa* 3.7)[34]

This clearly expresses the notion of an asymmetrical interpenetration of the human nature by the divine. Leonard Prestige glosses John Damascene's explanation of nature-perichoresis in the following way: 'The characteristics of the humanity [of Christ] are unimpaired, and its natural properties are unaltered. Nevertheless divine operations, though they do not proceed *from it*, do proceed *through it*, owing to the union and co-inherence.' That is, the human nature is the conduit through which the divine nature acts in the person of Christ. This sounds rather monophysite (the heresy that states Christ had only one *physis*, or nature). However, quoth Prestige,

---

[33] See *De fide orthodoxa* 3.4, and Richard Cross's article, 'Christological predication in John of Damascus', for a detailed exposition of John Damascene's views.

[34] John Damascene goes beyond this somewhat in a later portion of his treatise: 'The permeation [inhabitation, mutual indwelling] did not come of the flesh but of the divinity: for it is impossible that the flesh should permeate through the divinity: but the divine nature once permeating through the flesh gave also to the flesh the same ineffable power of permeation [*perichorousa*]; and this indeed is what we call union.' See *De fide orthodoxa* 4.18. All citations from *De fide orthodoxa* are taken from Salmond's translation in *The Nicene and Post-Nicene Fathers*, 2nd series, IX (Grand Rapids: Eerdmans, 1989 [reprint]).

John safeguards himself very carefully from Monophysitism. One result of the co-inherence of the two natures is an interchange or *antidosis*. But this is purely a matter of formality or nomenclature: no properties of either nature are actually transferred through it to the other, but the title derived from either nature may be applied to the Person in whom both natures are united.[35]

At first glance, this sounds like the communication of attributes once again. But it is not. The point Prestige is making is that, on Damascene's doctrine of nature-perichoresis, there is no transference of properties from one nature to another. The two natures remain distinct, unconfused and unmingled, exercising the properties that properly belong to them. The interpenetration of Christ's human nature by his divine nature is possible because this involves the exercise of one of the essential attributes of the divine nature, namely omnipresence. If Christ's divine nature is essentially omnipresent, then he must exist everywhere at once (however that is construed), interpenetrating all things that exist, including the human nature of Christ.[36] So there is an interpenetration of the human nature of Christ by the divine nature, which does not require the transfer of properties between natures and is asymmetrical in virtue of the omnipresence of the divine nature.[37]

---

[35] Prestige, 'ΠΕΡΙΧΟΡΕШ and ΠΕΡΙΧΟΡΕΣΙΣ in the Fathers', pp. 250 and 251 respectively (emphasis added). Compare Cross, who thinks Damascene is perfectly serious about a real union between the two natures of Christ: 'Christological predication in John of Damascus', p. 71.

[36] This is true even if, with Thomas (and other traditional perfect-being theologians), we deny that God is literally spatially located at every place. Thus Thomas: 'God is in all things by his power, inasmuch as all things are subject to His power; He is by His presence in all things, as all things are bare and open to His eyes; He is in all things by His essence, inasmuch as He is present to all as the cause of their being.' *Summa Theologiae* 1.8.3.

[37] The use of the term 'asymmetrical' in this context should be distinguished from the earlier use of the term 'unidirectional'. A unidirectional approach can lead to symmetry; for example, a (unidirectional) proposal of marriage may lead to the symmetry of becoming a spouse.

We are now in a position to summarize our findings regarding nature-perichoresis:

(1) The two natures of Christ subsist in a hypostatic union in the Incarnation.

(2) In this union there is a communication of properties between the divine nature and the human nature in the person of Christ.

Given that the strong version of the communication of attributes is fatally flawed, and that the moderate revision of the doctrine does not seem to apply to Christ's human nature prior to its glorification, I shall assume the weaker view, which is:

(3) The communication of attributes involves the attribution of the properties of each of the natures of Christ to the theanthropic person of Christ, such that the *person* of Christ is treated as having divine and human attributes at one and the same time, yet without predicating attributes of one nature that properly belong to the other nature in the hypostatic union, without transference of properties between the natures and without confusing or commingling the two natures of Christ or the generation of a *tertium quid*.

There is also a nature-perichoresis between the two natures of Christ, which is distinct from the communication of attributes. In order not to cause confusion about the nature of this relation between the two natures of Christ, I shall refer to this nature-perichoretic relation as penetration (of the human by the divine nature of Christ) in what follows, rather than as the *inter*penetration of each nature by the other. By this I mean that Christ's human nature is 'indwelt' by his divine nature in a way analogous to the indwelling of a human body by its soul (presuming human bodies have souls). I suppose that most substance-dualists would think the soul somehow 'indwells' or 'inhabits' the body, but the body does not 'inhabit' or 'indwell' the soul in the same way.[38] This is the sort of relation I have in view in the use of penetration. Interpenetration is a symmetrical sort of relation between two (or more) objects, since each object 'penetrates' the other. It is rather like the notion of two spatially overlapping objects. Suppose Tibbles is a cat with a tail, and Tibbs is the same hunk of matter as Tibbles but without Tibbles' tail. Both objects (assuming they are distinct objects) overlap, we might think, although they are distinct. Tibbles 'interpenetrates' Tibbs in some sense, and vice versa. But I do not think the same can be said for the relation between the divine and human natures of Christ, which is why I have opted for language of 'penetration' rather than 'inter-penetration', which would sound more theologically traditional in this sort of context.[39] We may now return to our summary of nature-perichoresis:

(4) The divine nature of Christ penetrates the human nature of Christ in virtue of divine omnipresence.

(5) This penetration is asymmetrical: the relation originates in the divine and moves in the direction of the human nature only. There is no sense in which the human nature penetrates the divine nature of Christ either in origination or reciprocation.

(6) Thus, in nature-perichoresis the two natures of Christ remain intact and unconfused. There is no transference of properties from one nature to the other. Nevertheless, there is a sense in

---

[38] Of course, an immaterial object cannot be said to 'indwell' anything, strictly speaking, because it is literally at no place, being without physical extension. But I presume that when we use such language of souls 'indwelling' bodies we use this language in an analogical, or 'stretched' sense. Just the same could be said of the use of penetration with respect to the hypostatic union.

[39] It would be an interesting project to see whether a more satisfying account of this perichoretic relation could be plotted than this merest of outlines. It seems to me that we are teetering on the edge of what can be said about these matters, and I could not go further into them here without a considerable detour from the matter in hand.

which we can speak of the penetration of the human by the divine nature of Christ.[40]

This does raise a question: In what sense is the perichoresis of the human nature of Christ by the divine nature of Christ anything more than the penetration of my human nature by the divine nature of God at each moment of my continued existence?

Earlier, I said that a difference of degree, rather than of kind, was important in distinguishing between these two sorts of penetration. That is, there is some way in which the intimacy of the hypostatic union means that the human nature of Christ is penetrated in a way that my human nature is not. Consider the following analogy, familiar in discussions of perichoresis. A sword could be said, in a loose and non-philosophical sense, to be 'penetrated' by the heat of the blacksmith's furnace as he forges the blade. (Of course, the sword is not literally penetrated by the heat of the furnace, but even if the relation involved in this example is something much weaker than penetration, the central point remains the same.) Presumably, if I were to place another sword in the furnace for a moment, it too would be 'penetrated' by the heat of the furnace and would become warm. But it would not be as hot as the first sword, which is being forged, and is a lot hotter than my own sword. The difference is one of quantity of heat, not quality of heat (both swords have been placed in the same furnace). But it is an important difference. One sword is red-hot, the other is merely warm. One sword will burn me if I touch it, the other will not, and so on.

Similarly, Christ's human nature may be penetrated in such a way in the hypostatic union that the difference between it and my nature on the question of penetration by the divine nature, while only a

---

[40] It might be thought that talk of 'penetration' in the sense I am using it here is misleading. All this actually means is that the divine nature is omnipresent in the human nature of Christ (in some special way). This is true. But in deference to the tradition, I shall continue to speak of this as perichoresis, although this may be a rather attenuated use of the term.

difference of degree, is, nevertheless, a significant degree of difference. For instance, Christ's consciousness of the (penetrative) presence of God would appear to have been significantly greater than most human beings. I am not consciously aware of God upholding and penetrating every fibre of my being at each moment of my existence. Nevertheless, he does so. But presumably, Christ was very much aware of this penetration of his human nature; for instance, he claimed that 'I and the Father are one' (John 10.30). More significantly, the penetration of my human nature by God does not enable me to perform miracles like walking on water, passing through walls or rising from the dead. But, I take it that on a classical Christology, this is exactly what the divine nature of Christ enables his human nature to do, via nature-perichoresis. (It could be argued that it is the Holy Spirit that enables the human nature of Christ to perform miracles, rather than Christ's divine nature, if, say, the divine nature of Christ is not thought to act in and through the human nature of Christ in this way during the Incarnation. But this is not a conventional view of the means by which Christ was able to perform miracles. A conventional view would claim that Christ was able to perform miracles in virtue of the action of his divine nature in and through his human nature in the hypostatic union.[41])

But does this activity of the divine nature in and through the human nature of Christ mean that *only* Christ could be acted upon in this way via nature-perichoresis? Is it not possible that God could enable me to walk on water, or to rise from the dead, through some increase of divine perichoretic activity in my own body? And if so, how is the nature-perichoresis experienced by Christ really different from the perichoresis I experience? The answer to these questions is simply this: God *could* act upon other human beings in the way in which he acts upon Christ. All that distinguishes the

---

[41] John Owen seems to have held the non-conventional view on this matter. See Alan Spence, 'Christ's humanity and ours: John Owen', in Christoph Schwöbel and Colin Gunton (eds.), *Persons, Divine and Human: King's College Essays in Theological Anthropology* (Edinburgh: T. & T. Clark, 1991).

perichoretic relation that Christ's human nature experiences with his divine nature, and that that my human nature experiences with God, is the degree to which the divine nature of Christ penetrates his human nature. But none of this means that there is not a difference between the way in which Christ's human nature is penetrated by the divine nature and the way in which I am penetrated by God.

Does this mean that the hypostatic union is redundant because God could have brought about the desired effect (person-perichoresis) by penetrating a human nature as he penetrates my human nature, without the need for a hypostatic union of two natures? Not necessarily. A number of classical theologians, following Anselm, say that the Incarnation *requires* there to be a divine and human nature in hypostatic union in the person of Christ.[42] If God were simply to create a human being, comprising a single human nature plus personhood, and to act upon that human being in a special way, via a non-hypostatic nature-perichoresis, this would not be sufficient for the purpose of the Incarnation. Such a person would not be both fully God and fully man. He would be fully man, but also only merely man, with only a human nature upon which God acts in a special way. This is the heresy of adoptionism. (Adoptionism states that Jesus of Nazareth was a human being who was 'adopted' or 'possessed' by the second person of the Trinity at some point in his life, becoming the Christ through this experience.)[43]

So, it seems to me that, although this version of nature-perichoresis does mean that the penetration of the human nature of Christ by his divine nature is different only in degree of divine inherence from that which is involved in God interpenetrating and upholding me at each moment of my existence, this nevertheless has important

---

[42] This, of course, is one of the central arguments in favour of the Incarnation offered by Anselm in *Cur Deus Homo.*

[43] There are other grounds upon which Christ's humanity is distinct from mine. His humanity is, according to classical theology, impeccable or at least, sinless; mine is peccable and sinful. His human nature is in hypostatic union with the divine nature; I am not. And so on.

ramifications in the doctrine of the Incarnation that do involve important differences between Christ and other human beings. And this need not lead away from orthodoxy. It also has the benefit of making sense of the communication of attributes and nature-perichoresis, and clearly distinguishes the one from the other.

Person-perichoresis

What then, of person-perichoresis? This, we shall see, presents quite different problems from nature-perichoresis.

In the recent theological literature, person-perichoresis has been used in an extravagant fashion, by theologians like Jürgen Moltmann, as a conceptual tool by which to make sense of social theories of the Trinity. For instance, Karen Kilby notes (somewhat ironically):

It is the divine perichoresis which makes the three one [in social theories of the Trinity], and it is perichoresis which makes the Trinity a wonderful doctrine. There is among the three divine persons, it is said, a kind of mutual interpenetration which is not to be found amongst human persons, and it is because of this perfect interpenetration that the three persons are one God.[44]

The use of person-perichoresis by theologians sympathetic to social theories of the Trinity (roughly, theories that emphasize the threeness rather than the oneness of the Trinity, often construed in terms of three divine individuals held together by a single divine essence, in which they participate perichoretically) does not mean that social-Trinity theorists have a monopoly on this version of perichoresis. It could be that a theologian defending an Augustinian account of the Trinity, whereby the persons of the Trinity are differentiated by relational properties alone, has as much reason to endorse a version

---

[44] Karen Kilby, 'Perichoresis and projection: problems with social doctrines of the Trinity', *New Blackfriars* 81 (2000), p. 435. For a short account of person-perichoresis in Moltmann's work, see his *The Trinity and the Kingdom of God*, trans. Margaret Kohl (London: SCM Press, 1981), pp. 174ff.

of person-perichoresis. This is precisely what I shall do. In this section of the book I shall assume an Augustinian doctrine of the Trinity as the model which informs my discussion of person-perichoresis.

To begin with, let us distinguish between properties (or, if one is a defender of divine simplicity, predicates) in the Trinity, belonging to individual persons of the Trinity, and properties that are shared between two or more persons of the Trinity.[45] Properties that are peculiar to one and only one person of the Trinity are called *proprietates* in scholastic theology. There are person-forming relations, fatherhood, sonship and (passive) spiration. There are also properties like 'being originless', which is said to belong to the Father alone as the 'source' of the Trinity. In addition to these distinguishing properties that belong to only one divine person, there are properties that are held by only two persons of the Trinity, such as the property of being the active spirator of the Spirit had by the Father and the Son, or, perhaps, the property of being a party to the decree of the covenant of redemption had by the Father and the Son. Anselm, standing foursquare in the Augustinian tradition of reflection upon the nature of the Trinity, makes an additional claim about the properties in the Trinity, to the effect that these properties can only be relational, and that there is a real distinction in the Trinity only where there is an opposition of the relations between two or more persons in the Trinity. This, according to Roman Catholic theologian Ludwig Ott, is called the basic Trinitarian law: *In God all is one where there is no opposition of relations.*[46]

We may now apply this to the doctrine of perichoresis. Ott explains that the Council of Florence in AD 1441 declared: 'Because of this unity the Father is wholly in the Son and wholly in the Holy Ghost, The Son is wholly in the Father and wholly in the Holy Ghost, the Holy

---

[45] This discussion of the distinguishing attributes of different persons of the Trinity is indebted to Ludwig Ott's discussion in *The Fundamentals of Catholic Dogma*, p. 70.

[46] Ibid. See also Anselm, *On the Procession of the Holy Spirit*, § 2, in *Anselm of Canterbury: The Major Works*, ed. Brian Davies and Gillian Evans (Oxford: Oxford University Press, 1998).

Ghost is wholly in the Father and wholly in the Son.'[47] The problem is how to make sense of this declaration in a way that does not end up occluding or overriding those divine attributes that pertain to only one person, or to only two persons, of the Trinity. For this reason, the following sort of notion of person-perichoresis is clearly inadequate:

The persons of the Trinity interpenetrate one another such that all the properties of each person of the Trinity are shared together in the essence of the Godhead.

Let us call this the *Strong Person-perichoresis Thesis*, or SPT. The SPT is compatible with the declaration of the Council of Florence, but it is false, for several reasons.

First, it cannot be the case that each of the persons of the Trinity shares all the same properties because, as we have already seen, there are at least two sorts of properties which are not held in common in the Godhead. These are properties that are possessed by one and only one of the persons of the Trinity. For instance, the property 'possessing underived being' is a property of the Father alone. It is metaphysically impossible that either of the other two persons of the Trinity possess this property. Then there are properties that belong to only two persons of the Trinity, such as 'actively spirating the Holy Spirit'. Such properties, like those relational properties that are shared between the three persons of the Godhead (e. g. 'being one of the persons of the divine Trinity'), are necessarily true of God. That is, there is no possible world in which God does not possess these properties.[48] This means that there are properties which are necessary

---

47 Ott, *The Fundamentals of Catholic Dogma*, p. 71. Protestant theologians may not believe themselves to be bound by the findings of this council. Nevertheless, it expresses the doctrine of nature-perichoresis in an elegant fashion, and is taken to be a standard expression of this doctrine in the tradition.

48 Hence, they are neither 'hard' nor 'soft' properties in the sense that Swinburne uses in *The Christian God* (Oxford: Oxford University Press, 1994), p. 35. The question of whether God has these necessary properties timelessly or temporally is beyond the scope of the current discussion.

to the Godhead, but which are not shared by all the persons of the Godhead, in which case, SPT folds.

Secondly, the SPT is false because it entails a contradiction: God cannot both be triune *and* subsist in three persons who share *all the same* properties as each other; the reason being that this falls foul of the principle of the identity of indiscernibles. To recap, this is the notion that a thing is identical to another thing just in case that thing has all the same properties as the first thing. So, Tweedledum 1 is identical to Tweedledum 2 just in case Tweedledum 1 has all the same properties as Tweedledum 2. And if Tweedledum 1 is identical with Tweedledum 2 at any one time, then he is identical with Tweedledum 2 at all times, since, by virtue of the necessity of identity, if a thing is identical with another thing at one time, it must be identical with that thing at every other time at which it exists. For a thing must be identical with itself at all times. So, if the SPT obtains, then God cannot be triune and subsist in three persons, because, on SPT, there are no properties that might individuate the persons of the Trinity. For there are no properties which one, and only one, person of the Trinity possesses on SPT. This, in turn, means there can be no distinct, divine persons to speak of. For distinct persons require distinct properties in order to individuate them. But there can be no such properties, given SPT. So there can be no distinct divine persons, on SPT. And if there are no persons, there is no Trinity. Hence, the SPT leads to the denial of the Trinity.

But it might be thought that the persons of the Godhead could be individuated in virtue of haecceity, or 'thisness', rather than in virtue of any properties that they possess.[49] And if this is true, then even if two individuals share all the same properties, they could still be different individuals, distinguished by the fact that each one is 'this'

---

[49] Haecceity is, roughly, the property a particular thing has in virtue of being 'that thing' rather than some other thing. This entails that a particular object has thisness only if it is self-identical, e.g. Jones is self-identical with Jones = Jones is 'this' ('Jonesian') thing. See E. J. Lowe, *A Survey of Metaphysics* (Oxford: Oxford University Press, 2003), p. 102.

individual rather than 'that' individual. But, it could be argued that it is not the case that the divine persons are individuated solely on the basis of thisness, because God has properties that are metaphysically necessary and which are peculiar to only one person of the Trinity. In which case, for the second person of the Trinity to be instantiated, that person must have certain properties, like 'being the Son'. Since it is metaphysically necessary that the second person of the Trinity have this property, and since it is impossible for the second person of the Trinity to fail to exist, the second person of the Trinity must have this property. This property and others serve to individuate the second person from the other persons of the Trinity. So, thisness is not an option for individuating the persons of the Trinity. Richard Swinburne takes a similar view at one point in his discussion of this divine nature. He claims that a divine nature lacks thisness because 'there is nothing more to a divine individual than the instantiation of the divine essence and any further individuating relational properties (e.g. 'being begotten')'.[50]

So, some alternative to SPT has to be found which takes into account the fact that the relation involved in person-perichoresis applies equally to each of the divine persons and makes sense of those properties that are not shared in the divine life of the Godhead. Unlike nature-perichoresis, where the relation involved is asymmetrical and involves the penetration of the human nature by the divine nature in virtue of omnipresence, the unity of the Godhead demands that the perichoretic relation involved expresses an even more intimate relationship than this. So a more robust notion of perichoresis has to be found that can meet this requirement for the coinherence of the persons of the Trinity. For instance:

The persons of the Trinity share all their properties in a common divine essence apart from those properties that serve to individuate each person of the Trinity, or express a relation between only two persons of the Trinity.

[50] Swinburne, *The Christian God*, p. 189.

Call this the *Weak Person-perichoresis Thesis*, or WPT. On this version of person-perichoresis the interpenetration of each of the persons of the Trinity by the others is limited, rather than complete. But this, it seems to me, is a requirement for a doctrine of person-perichoresis that makes sense, otherwise the individuation of the persons of the Trinity is jeopardized.

Is this WPT compatible with the decree of the Council of Florence? Recall that the Council's formula was:

> Because of this unity the Father is wholly in the Son and wholly in the Holy Ghost, the Son is wholly in the Father and wholly in the Holy Ghost, the Holy Ghost is wholly in the Father and wholly in the Son.

The answer is that our formulation of person-perichoresis is compatible with the Council's decree only if the phrase 'wholly in x' is understood to mean something like 'wholly in x, yet exclusive of individuating properties and properties shared between only two persons of the Trinity'. This is rather an awkward way of reading the decree. But it seems to me that something like this is required in order to preserve the requirement of relational properties that individuate the persons of the Trinity.

Conclusions

To sum up: although some of the Fathers were not entirely clear about the matter, we need to distinguish between the communication of attributes and nature-perichoresis. In the former, contrary to the strong Lutheran view of the matter, there is no bilateral transfer of properties from one nature to the other. It may be that Christ's glorified human nature does share certain properties with the divine nature (with the exception of omnipresence). But, for the purposes of describing the non-glorified human nature of Christ, the communication of attributes is merely a device by which we may refer to both natures of Christ via the person of Christ in phrases like Christ's declaration: 'Before Abraham was born, I am.'

Nature-perichoresis (pre-glorification) is something more than this. But here, too, caution must be exercised. There is only the penetration of the human by the divine nature, and only in terms of the omnipresence of the divine nature (and without omnipresence being transferred to the human nature in the process). This is similar in kind, but not in degree, to the way in which God penetrates all created things. Person-perichoresis is different from nature-perichoresis in this regard. In person-perichoresis, the divine persons share most but not all divine properties together in the divine essence. Thus, person-perichoresis must be robust enough to express this strong sense of interpenetration required for the Trinity to make sense. But it must also be fine-grained enough to ensure that it does not obscure or deny the fact that there are properties that individuate the persons of the Trinity that are not shared together in this perichoresis.

None of this actually gives a *complete explanation* of what perichoresis is. What does it mean for the human nature of Christ to be penetrated by the omnipresence of the divine nature of Christ to a greater degree than the way in which the divine nature penetrates me? And what does it mean to say that the three persons of the Trinity interpenetrate one another in their shared life together, while remaining, at one and the same time, one God in three distinct persons? I cannot say because I do not know. This is a divine mystery before which theology must give way to doxology.

2 | The human nature of Christ

> For the 'Word made flesh' [John 1:14] assumed another nature, not another person. For when we speak of 'human being', we signify only the nature that is common to all human beings.
>
> St Anselm of Canterbury

In the previous chapter we discussed an issue that focused on the divinity and humanity of Christ as the first of three chapters laying out central aspects of a Chalcedonian Christology. Perichoresis in the Incarnation has to do with the way in which the hypostatic union of Christ's two natures are united in such an intimate fashion that the divinity of Christ because of his omnipresence penetrates the humanity of Christ, but the converse is not the case. Thus we have one person, in whom divinity and humanity are united, as the creed says, 'without confusion or mixture'.

This chapter and the next are two parts of a larger whole. In these two chapters we shall consider a second area where issues pertaining to the humanity and divinity of Christ are important. This has to do with the human nature assumed by the second person of the Trinity in the Incarnation. Discussion of this topic has a long and convoluted history in Christian thinking, much of which has to do with what is denoted by 'nature' and 'person' in the hypostatic union.[1] We shall focus our attention upon what Christ's human nature consists in and

---

[1] Compare John Meyendorff, *Christ in Eastern Christian Thought* (Crestwood: St Vladimir's Press, 1975), ch. 1. On the flesh of Christ: 'the biblical notion of flesh ("the Word was made flesh" John 1.14) had lost in the Greek world its original sense of animated creature and was largely used as a synonym of body in opposition to the

apply our findings to several longstanding theological problems for the Incarnation.

This chapter proceeds in three stages. The first lays out some of the historical-theological context for the discussion, and takes issue with one well-known story about the parties involved in pre-Chalcedonian Christology. The second lays out a taxonomy of different views on the human nature of Christ. The object of this exercise is to make some sense of the different views of Christ's human nature one could take, which is often left undone in discussions of this aspect of Christology. The third stage considers which of these different views of Christ's human nature are theologically orthodox. In trying to navigate this course, we shall have to avoid the Scylla and Charybdis of Apollinarianism and Nestorianism, two heresies with which differing views of Christ's human nature are sometimes charged. It will be apparent from this assessment that some of these views seem monothelitic, that is, they seem to imply that Christ had only one will. This is a problem for several reasons, including the fact that the Sixth Ecumenical Council of Constantinople repudiated monothelitism in AD 681. There are also those notions of Christ's human nature that imply dyothelitism (that Christ had two wills), which was affirmed by the same ecumenical council. The upshot of this is that, although a range of views is commensurate with the *letter* of the Chalcedonian definition of Christology, some sit less easily with the construal of Chalcedonianism laid out at Constantinople in AD 681. This is important if the understanding of Chalcedon given by the Fathers of the Third Council of Constantinople is thought to be the legitimate development of the Christological insights of the earlier council. It seems to me that someone dissenting from the findings of an ecumenical council of the Church should have a very good reason – indeed, a very good *theological* reason – for doing so. I can think of no good theological reason for rejecting the findings of the Third

---

soul' (p. 20). On nature: 'The term "nature" always indicated a concrete reality, and, at times, a personal reality' (p. 16). Cf. p. 26.

Council of Constantinople.[2] This leads me to prefer dyothelite views of Christ's human nature to the monothelite views.[3]

The historical-theological context

In textbooks of the history of Christian doctrine it is often said that there were, prior to the Council of Chalcedon, two main schools of Christology, associated with the theological centres of Alexandria

---

[2] It is interesting that many of the current discussions of Christology in philosophical theology tend to reject the Constantinopolitan construal of Chalcedon for philosophical, rather than theological, reasons, e.g., 'We cannot make metaphysical sense of one person with two wills.' But this does not seem to me to be a sufficient reason for rejecting the findings of the Constantinopolitan Fathers. After all, the hypostatic union is a mystery. The fact that we cannot make sense of this does not necessarily mean it is nonsense. It just means it is beyond our ken. A good theological reason for rejecting a conciliar decree would be that it conflicts with Scripture. But, as far as I can see, this does not apply in the present case.

[3] In the course of this chapter, I shall refer to a number of theological positions as unorthodox. I take it that a doctrine is unorthodox if it either (a) contradicts the teaching of Scripture (e.g. 'Jesus of Nazareth is not the Son of God') or (b) entails some doctrine that has been repudiated by an ecumenical council of the Church (e.g. 'God is not triune'). On my understanding, a view is not unorthodox just because a particular denomination or ecclesial community denies it. That is, denial by a certain ecclesial community is not a sufficient reason for rejecting a doctrine as unorthodox. (E.g., the *filioque* clause of the Western version of the Nicene-Constantinopolitan creed is affirmed by Roman Catholics and Protestants, but denied by the Orthodox. This clause states that the Holy Spirit is the one *qui ex patre et filioque procedit*, that is, who proceeds from the Father *and the Son*. The Orthodox deny the phrase 'and the Son'.) Nor is it any part of my argument that certain theological doctrines are unorthodox simply because *I think they are*, or because *I do not like them*. My concern is simply to show whether or not certain views on the human nature of Christ are consistent with the teaching of Scripture and the ecumenical councils of the Church. (Although I shall argue only for the latter, I presume that any Christian doctrine must be compatible with Holy Writ.) Someone could hold to unorthodox views and not be a heretic. For instance, Smith might believe that the Bible is not the Word of God, which (as I understand it) is an implicit denial of 2 Tim. 3.16. But this, on its own, is not sufficient for Smith to be considered heretical, or outside the bounds of the Church or salvation. So, as I am using the term, unorthodoxy is weaker than heresy. I will say nothing about the nature of heresy in this chapter.

and Antioch.[4] According to this story, Chalcedon represents a compromise statement that attempted to grant something to both of these competing approaches to Christology in an effort to foreclose further argument. Not surprisingly, it failed to satisfy all the different parties involved.[5] These two schools, the Alexandrian and Antiochene, are often characterized in the following way. The Alexandrians emphasized the unity of the person of Christ and his divinity, characterized by the slogan 'logos-sarx (Word-Flesh) Christology', because it is the Word who assumes the flesh of human nature at the Incarnation. But this does not mean that the Word takes on a human soul distinct from the Word. Were this to occur, so the Alexandrians averred, the result would not be the assumption of human nature by the Word, but the assumption of a human person by the Word. We might call it *divine possession* rather than *divine Incarnation*. That is, if the Word assumed a human soul distinct from his divine nature, he would be assuming or possessing an existing concrete particular, rather than assuming human nature, and this is (one aspect of) the heresy of Nestorianism. (This heresy says that the Word assumed an existing person, indwelling and coexisting with him for the duration of the Incarnation.[6]) In order to guard against this, Alexandrian

---

4 For a brief overview of these matters, see Daniel Migliore's introduction to systematic theology, *Faith Seeking Understanding*, 2nd edn (Grand Rapids: Eerdmans, 2004 [1991]), pp. 169–173; Jaroslav Pelikan, *The Christian Tradition*, I: *The Emergence of the Catholic Tradition (100–600)* (Chicago: University of Chicago Press, 1971), ch. 5; and Otto Weber, *Foundations of Dogmatics*, II, trans. Darrell L. Guder (Grand Rapids: Eerdmans, 1983), pp. 111–114.

5 For the view that Chalcedon leaned in the direction of Alexandrian Christology, see Alvin Plantinga, 'On heresy, mind, and truth' *Faith and Philosophy* 16/2 (1999), p. 185. For the view that Chalcedon leaned towards the Antiochene position, see Robert Jenson, *Systematic Theology*, I: *The Triune God* (New York: Oxford University Press, 1997), ch. 8. A good account of the differing post-Chalcedonian parties is given by John Meyendorff, *Christ in Eastern Christian Thought*, ch. 2.

6 See Thomas, *Summa Contra Gentiles* 4.34. Compare H. J. Schroeder, OP, *Disciplinary Decrees of the General Councils: Text, Translation, and Commentary* (London: Herder Books, 1937), pp. 70ff.; G. Leonard Prestige, *Fathers and Heretics* (London: SPCK, 1954), Lecture VI; and Donald Macleod, *The Person of Christ* (Leicester: Inter-Varsity

theologians denied that the Word's assumption of human nature entails the assumption of a human soul distinct from and in addition to his divine nature. The limiting case of this sort of Christology is the heresy of Apollinarianism, which states that Christ had no human soul, its place being taken by the Word.[7]

The other school of Christology, the Antiochene, emphasized the humanity of Christ and the distinction between the two natures in the hypostatic union. The Antiochenes are often characterized by the phrase '*logos-anthropos* (Word-human being) Christology'. According to this view, the human soul assumed by the Word is distinct from the divine Word. But, as we shall see, this should not be taken to mean that the Word assumes a fully formed and already existing human being. Rather, he assumes a human body and human soul at the moment of incarnation – the moment at which this

Press, 1998), chs. 6 and 7. Nestorius may not have been a Nestorian. Whether or not Nestorius was a Nestorian is distinct from the question of whether the view that is called Nestorianism is a heresy, which it is. According to Nestorianism, the Word indwells Christ to a greater degree than in most other human beings, but not in a different kind of way from other human beings. This sounds rather like the version of nature-perichoresis defended in the previous chapter. The crucial difference between these two views is that nature-perichoresis requires the doctrine of the hypostatic union that Nestorianism denies. It is also worth pointing out that Nestorianism entails adoptionism, the view that the Word 'adopts' an existing human being, but is not entailed by it.

[7] In fact, things are a little more complex than this, for two reasons. First, it has often been claimed that this was only one of the heretical propositions affirmed by Apollinarius. The other was that Christ's body was not human; it was not assumed from Mary *Theotokos*. Instead, it was formed out of the divine essence. But this is disputed among patristic scholars. Second, strictly speaking, Apollinarius affirmed that 'there was a sensitive soul in Christ; nonetheless, it was without mind and intellect, so that the Word of God was in that soul in place of intellect and mind'. Thomas, *Summa Contra Gentiles* 4.33, 4.31–32. See Charles E. Raven, *Apollinarianism: An Essay on the Christology of the Early Church* (Cambridge: Cambridge University Press, 1923), and H. J. Schroeder, *Disciplinary Decrees of the General Councils*, p. 64. It is ironic that Apollinarius was a champion of Nicene Christianity, but shared with Arius the belief that the Word did not possess a human mind.

human nature is created by the work of the Holy Spirit. The limiting case of Antiochene Christology is the Nestorian claim that there are two persons in Christ, the divine person 'indwelling' the human.

There is certainly something to be said for this historical story about the development of Alexandrian and Antiochene Christology. But it may be a little too neat, as a cursory glance at the work of St Cyril of Alexandria shows. In developing his own view against Nestorius, Cyril says: 'It would seem to be the proper conclusion that the one assumed in this inseparable union has become the personal property of the one assuming.'

This seems to imply that the human nature of Christ is a property that is assumed by the Word, rather than some concrete particular consisting of a human body and distinct human soul that the Word assumes. However, a little later in the same work he affirms: 'We say that there is one Son, and that he has one nature even when he is considered as having assumed flesh endowed with a rational soul. As I have already said, he has made the human element his own. And this is the way, not otherwise, that we must consider that the same one is at once God and man.'[8] Here it sounds as if the human nature of Christ is a human body with a 'rational' human soul distinct from the Word. And this seems much more in keeping with the Antiochene tradition, rather than with the Alexandrian. There are other, related problems with interpreting Cyril that one could appeal to here. For instance, he appears to use the term 'nature' to refer to that which is united in the hypostatic union (what would now be called the person of Christ) and, at other times, to mean the divine and human natures of Christ. (This, according to John Meyendorff, is how the post-Chalcedonian monophysites understood Cyril.[9]) So, it appears

---

[8] St Cyril of Alexandria, *On the Unity of Christ*, trans. John Anthony McGuckin (Crestwood: St Vladimir's Press, 2000), pp. 75 and 77 respectively.
[9] See Meyendorff, *Christ in Eastern Christian Thought*, p. 29.

that Cyril, usually taken to be the doyen of Alexandrian Christology, is not always *unambiguously* Alexandrian, in the way relevant to this theological story about the development of pre-Chalcedonian Christology.[10]

My point, then, is that the history that informs this account of the conflict between two clear-cut positions on the person of Christ, represented by the Alexandrians and the Antiochenes, is not as straightforward as it might at first appear. It may be that there are discernible traditions of Christology associated with Alexandria and Antioch, and that these loose 'schools' of thought shared a number of common convictions and ideas about the way in which the Incarnation should be understood. But I am less convinced that this story, as it stands, is an adequate account of the ideological cut-and-thrust that went on between the different theologians in the pre-Chalcedonian (or even post-Chalcedonian) debate about the person of Christ. For this reason, I shall not make any claims about whether one or other of the two views on the person of Christ this chapter deals with is strictly representative of one particular theological school in the early Church. That said, I think the two views I shall outline are representative of two ways of thinking about the human nature of Christ that can be found in the Christian tradition and are often thought of as representing a broadly 'Alexandrian' or 'Antiochene' Christology. And, for the record, the view defended in this chapter falls quite clearly within the boundaries of 'Antiochene', rather than 'Alexandrian', Christology.

---

[10] I give this as one example. As anyone familiar with the literature on patristic theology will know, it is often the case that the disputes among different participants in the early Christological debates is convoluted and seldom as clearly defined as modern textbooks might suggest. Part of the problem is that the very vocabulary of Christology was being thrashed out in these discussions, and this often meant one writer developing the use of certain technical terms that were not understood in the same way by all participants. Charles Raven makes this point in his discussion of Apollinarius, his critics and the influence his theology had in later theological discussion. See *Apollinarianism*, chs. VI–VII.

Different views on the human nature of Christ

In the course of his discussion of the Incarnation, Thomas opines that '*nature* is a word used in many ways.'[11] This is certainly true. In the current literature, several terminologies are used to distinguish different sorts of views about the human nature of Christ.[12] Some philosophical theologians speak of concrete- and abstract-nature views of the human nature of Christ. A concrete-nature view is one that states that Christ's human nature is a concrete particular, perhaps a human body, but, traditionally, a human body and human soul distinct from the Word. An abstract-nature view says that Christ's human nature is a property, or set of properties, necessary and sufficient for being human. (Of course, any particular human being will have other properties besides those requisite for being human, properties that are peculiar to that individual. In the case of Christ, these properties include things like 'being born in Bethlehem in a manger in 4 BC', 'being the God-Man', and so forth.[13])

There are also what we might call 'parts' Christologies, according to which Christ is composed of a number of 'parts', usually two or three parts.[14] Two-part Christologies state that Christ is composed of

---

[11] *Summa Contra Gentiles* 4.41.2.

[12] Some of the most metaphysically sophisticated accounts of Christ's human nature can be found in medieval theology, a veritable smorgasbord of different views on this subject that we cannot go into here. Happily, this has been done elsewhere. See, for example, Richard Cross's excellent study, *The Metaphysics of the Incarnation*, and Heiko Oberman's *The Harvest of Medieval Theology*, 3rd edn (Grand Rapids: Baker, 2000).

[13] Compare Plantinga, who uses the abstract- and concrete-nature distinction: 'The second person of the Trinity acquired the property of being human; he acquired whatever property it is that is necessary and sufficient for being human. (Of course he also had properties no other human has or has had, and even properties no other human being could have had, just as you or I do.) The human nature he assumed, then, was a property.' 'On heresy, mind, and truth', p. 183.

[14] Brian Leftow makes use of this distinction in 'A timeless God Incarnate', in Stephen Davis, Daniel Kendall and Gerald O'Collins (eds.), *The Incarnation* (Oxford: Oxford University Press, 2002), p. 29. See also Cross, *The Metaphysics of the Incarnation*. If one

two 'parts', the Word and a human body.[15] The Word either possesses the property of being a human soul in relation to this body, from the Incarnation onwards, or stands in the relation to this human body that a soul does. Three-part Christologies say that Christ has three 'parts': the Word, and a human nature comprising a body-and-soul composite, distinct from the Word. (I shall not delve into the question of whether or not the 'parts' involved in these two ways of thinking about the Incarnation are proper parts of the Word, or whether they are just a convenient way of thinking about the different 'aspects' of God Incarnate. Defenders of a traditional view of divine simplicity, the doctrine that denies that God has any parts whatsoever, would resist talk of real metaphysical 'parts' pertaining to the person of Christ. Since it would be impractical to make this point clear every time we refer to 'parts' Christologies, readers sympathetic to a traditional account of divine simplicity should make the relevant mental qualification hereinafter when reading of 'two-' or 'three-part' Christologies.[16])

Matters are complicated by the fact that these two ways of thinking about the human nature of Christ overlap in important respects, but are nevertheless distinct. Consider the case of the abstract-nature view. A particular theologian could hold that Christ's human nature

thinks that human persons are material beings, like Peter van Inwagen, then Christ is composed of the Word and a human body (still a two-'part' Christology). But without some argument, this seems straightforwardly Apollinarian. Could Christ be composed of only one 'part'? I cannot see how. Christ must have at least two 'parts': his divine nature and a human nature.

[15] In distinguishing between the human nature of Christ and his pre-existing divine nature, I shall often speak of the Word and his human nature, or the human nature he assumes at the Incarnation.

[16] For two recent accounts that deal with this question, see Christopher Hughes, *On a Complex Theory of a Simple God: An Investigation in Aquinas' Philosophical Theology* (Ithaca: Cornell University Press, 1989), ch. 7, and John Lamont, 'The nature of the hypostatic union', *Heythrop Journal* 47 (2006), pp. 16–25. I suppose that even defenders of divine simplicity would have to concede that Christ's human nature has physical parts, e.g. hands, feet and so forth. Quite how, or even whether, one could square this with divine simplicity is beyond the scope of this chapter.

is an abstract object, a property, and that the Incarnation is just the assumption, or the exemplification, of this particular property by the Word in addition to those properties he has that are essential to his divine nature. This way of thinking about the abstract-nature view of the Incarnation involves a realist theory of properties, where properties are thought to be abstract objects that are universals that particular objects exemplify. Take one common example, the universal 'redness', exemplified by the red ball, the red jacket or the red tomato. (*How* red things exemplify redness need not detain us here.) This is not the only way of making sense of the idea that Christ's human nature is not fundamentally a concrete object. The obvious alternative would be a version of nominalism with respect to predicates or particulars (as opposed to properties that are universals). Then, there are no universals to which particulars correspond, or, more precisely, which particulars exemplify. There are different versions of nominalist theories about particulars just as there are different realist theories about properties, and this is not the place to present a comprehensive survey of different views on this subject in current metaphysics. But one nominalist theory about particulars that looks to me like an obvious candidate for theologians thinking about the human nature of Christ is *trope* theory. According to this view (or family of views), particulars are abstract objects, in fact, properties; but they are not universals. Instead, they are properties possessed by individual concrete things, such as string, sealing-wax, cabbages and kings. So, for a trope theorist, the redness of the ball is just the redness that *this particular* ball has, just as the redness of the jacket or of the tomato is the redness of *that particular* jacket or *that particular* tomato.[17] It is not the case that each red thing is an instance of some universal 'redness' that each exemplifies in some

---

[17] Indeed, one might be a trope theorist who thinks all that individual concrete objects consist of are bundles of particulars. Then a particular tomato is just a bundle of properties including the redness of this tomato, the roundness of this tomato, and so forth. Or one might think that there are tropes and bare particulars that exemplify them, in a way similar to John Locke.

way. Applied to the Incarnation, this would mean that the human nature of Christ is a property of a particular sort (no pun intended). In other words, Christ does not exemplify some property (human nature) common to all human beings, in the Incarnation. In assuming human nature he takes on something that only this particular individual, Christ, has (but which other instances of human nature have in a precisely parallel way), just as the redness of a given tomato is particular to that tomato. So, the defender of a view of the Incarnation sympathetic to the idea that properties are tropes could say that Christ's human nature is the property particular to the Word, or the property that the Word has from the Incarnation onwards. This trope theory could count as a version of the abstract-nature view of Christ's humanity because trope theorists do not deny that particulars are abstract objects of a sort; they merely deny that they are universals. (Of course, there are other nominalist views that this would not be true of. I shall not deal with any of these views, although I suppose someone could take a nominalist view of Christ's human nature other than a trope theory.)

The abstract-nature view of the Incarnation could be taken according to either a two- or a three-part Christology. This point is sometimes overlooked, with the result that abstract-nature views are often thought of as equivalent to two-part Christologies of some kind. But it is not the only way of thinking about an abstract-nature view. The property or conjunctive property of Christ's human nature could include 'having a human body' and 'having a human soul', where the soul in question is distinct from the Word. Or the property of human nature could just be such that Christ has the property of having a human body and being a human soul in addition to being the Word. In which case, the Word would not have a human soul in addition to his divine nature. In a similar way, if I have an extra limb grafted on to my body, one might think that I persist through that change to my physical parts, although I gain a physical part after the graft that I did not have prior to the graft. Then, I have the property of having an extra limb that I did not possess prior to the procedure that grafted this extra limb on to my body. The Incarnation, on this way of thinking about the abstract-nature view, is consistent with a two-part construal of Christ's theanthropic (God-Man) person. Prior to the Incarnation, the Word did not have the property of being a human soul; after the Incarnation he does have this property.[18] From that moment onwards, he is a human soul contingently, but remains a divine person essentially. And of course, one could take either a two-part or a three-part view of the Incarnation coupled with the idea that the human nature of Christ is a universal, or couple either of these two- and three-part views with the idea that Christ's human nature is a particular of some sort, depending on what one believes about the existence of abstract objects. The upshot of this is that it is possible to think of Christ's human nature as an abstract object in several quite different ways.

The same sort of reasoning applies, *mutatis mutandis*, to the concrete-nature view. Someone who advocates this way of thinking about the human nature of Christ could say that it is a body–soul composite of some sort. Then, we have a three-part Christology (Word + human body + human soul). Alternatively, one could claim that Christ's human nature is a human body, the Word taking the place of a human soul. Then we would have a concrete-nature view that yields a two-part Christology, the two parts being the Word

---

[18] Alternatively, it could be argued that the Word always has the property of being a human soul in addition to having a divine nature, although possession of this property of being a human soul is had contingently. This seems to be the view of William Lane Craig and J. P. Moreland in their book *Philosophical Foundations for a Christian Worldview* (Downers Grove, IL: InterVarsity Press, 2003), ch. 30. But this seems Apollinarian. See John Anthony McGuckin, *The Westminster Handbook to Patristic Theology* (Louisville: Westminster John Knox Press, 2004), entry 'Apollinaris of Laodicea', pp. 21–22. 'The Logos', according to Apollinarius, 'constituted humans as the image of God. The image was particularly located in the *nous*, the spiritual intellect. This was also the seat of personhood (mind and soul). In the case of Jesus the Logos did not need to assume a human mind (logos or rationality), as he himself was the archetype of all intellect. In this one case the image was not anthropologically needed as the original was present, replacing it.'

and the human body of Christ. The problem for this version of a concrete-nature view is that it is straightforwardly Apollinarian (that is, it entails, as it stands, that Christ had no human soul, the Word taking the place that a human soul would normally take in a body–soul composite). Such a two-part concrete-nature view of the Incarnation should be distinguished from abstract-nature views that state that the Word assumes the property of having a human body and the property of being a human soul, or views like this that do not yield an Apollinarian conclusion. (We shall return to this issue later in the chapter.)

It is also important to see that, as with the abstract-nature view, advocates of concrete-nature views of the Incarnation (taken according to either a two- or a three-part Christology) could be realists or nominalists about properties. The important difference between concrete- and abstract-nature views of Christ's humanity on this matter is that the advocate of a concrete-nature view thinks that the human nature of Christ is a concrete particular assumed by the Word, not just a property possessed by the Word. Naturally, the human nature of Christ still has properties on the concrete-nature view, but what is of fundamental importance is that the human nature of Christ is a concrete particular, whereas, it seems, what is fundamental to abstract-nature views is that the human nature of Christ is a property. (This is not to deny that defenders of the abstract-nature view think that Christ has a corporeal body, or that Jesus of Nazareth is a concrete particular.) So, according to the defender of a concrete-nature view, Christ's human nature is first and foremost a concrete particular that has certain properties, not a property of the Word that entails possession of a certain concrete particular. The defender of a concrete-nature view of Christ's human nature will say that it is a mistake to think that Christ's human nature is fundamentally a property. And, of course, the same applies, vice versa: those committed to an abstract-nature view of Christ's humanity will regard it as a mistake to think that human nature is fundamentally a concrete particular.

Apart from the obviously Apollinarian two-part, concrete-nature view of the Incarnation, the ways of thinking about Christ's human nature that we have examined all seem to be compatible with Chalcedonian Christology, where this means 'compatible with what the Chalcedonian definition states is orthodox Christian belief'. None of them is obviously unorthodox; they are all compatible with a two-natures doctrine of the Incarnation and do not end up confusing or conflating one nature with another (while taking very different views of what this human nature is). Nevertheless, there is an important distinction between these differing positions that has to do with dyothelitism. According to the Sixth Ecumenical Council of the Church in Constantinople (AD 680–681), there are two wills and two centres of action in Christ, but not two persons:

> We likewise declare that in him [Christ] are two natural wills (*dyo physikas theleseis*) and two natural operations (*dyo physikas energeias*) indivisibly, inconvertibly, inseparably, inconfusedly, according to the teaching of the holy Fathers. And these two natural wills are not contrary the one to the other (God forbid!) as the impious heretics assert, but his human will follows and that not as resisting and reluctant, but rather as subject to his divine and omnipotent will.[19]

The Third Council of Constantinople was convened to attempt to bring some clarity to the controversy surrounding monothelitism (the idea that Christ had only one, divine, will). This view was developed in the forlorn hope of reconciling monophysites alienated by Chalcedon, who, like Apollinarius, taught that Christ had one (divine) nature, not two (divine and human). But monothelitism was regarded as a betrayal of Chalcedon by a number of theologians, including Maximus the Confessor, whose work carried the day for dyothelitism at Constantinople. This controversy, and the particular

---

[19] Translated by Henry R. Percival in *The Seven Ecumenical Councils of the Undivided Church: Their Canons and Dogmatic Decrees* (New York: Edwin S. Gorham, 1901), p. 345.

doctrine advocated by Maximus, is beyond the scope of this chapter.[20] But it is worth pointing out that the Fathers of the Third Council of Constantinople felt that their development of Chalcedonian Christology was in the spirit of Chalcedon in a way that monothelitism, with an eye towards reconciling the monophysites, was not.

Be that as it may, some recent philosophical theologians, believing that possession of two wills implies two persons rather than two natures in one person, argue that an abstract-nature view of Christ's human nature is preferable to a concrete-nature view, despite the fact that it seems monothelite.[21] An advocate of such a two-part Christology could still claim to be Chalcedonian. After all, it could be argued, the monothelite controversy did not make its way into conciliar documents until AD 681, fully 230 years after the Chalcedonian definition was drafted. Taken at face value (and without the historical development of the Chalcedonian position in the canons of Constantinople in AD 681), it could be thought that an abstract-nature view that implies monothelitism is still orthodox because it is consistent with the letter of the Chalcedonian definition, which says nothing about whether Christ had one or two wills. But this seems unsatisfactory, not least because it means pitting the canons of one ecumenical council against another. Why accept the decree of Chalcedon and not the decree of the Third Council of Constantinople? If it is thought that the authority of one ecumenical council is not on a par with another, then some argument has to be given as to why this is the case. It is no good simply choosing one and rejecting the

[20] According to Andrew Louth, Maximus distinguished between willing something where there is deliberation between alternatives, including sinful alternatives (*gnomic willing*) and *natural willing*, where it is of the nature of a particular being to have the disposition to will things. Christ has a human will only in this latter sense. Thus Maximus: 'The Incarnate Word possesses as a human being the natural disposition to will, and this is moved and shaped by the divine will.' *Opusculum 3*, 48A, cited in Louth, *Maximus the Confessor* (London: Routledge, 1996), pp. 61 and 193.

[21] For instance, William Lane Craig and J. P. Moreland in *Philosophical Foundations for a Christian Worldview*, ch. 30. I am not suggesting that commitment to an abstract-nature view of the humanity of Christ *entails* monothelitism.

mean that the Word becomes a material object (something which lantinga explicitly rejects). What is assumed at the Incarnation is aken on *in addition to*, not *in place of*, his divine nature. Athanasius of Alexandria makes a similar point:

> For he was not, as might be imagined, circumscribed in the body, nor, while present in the body, was he absent elsewhere; nor, while he moved the body, was the universe left void of his working and providence; but, thing most marvellous, Word as he was, so far from being contained by anything, he rather contained all things himself; and just as while present in the whole of creation, he is at once distinct in being from the universe, and present in all things by his own power . . . thus, even while present in a human body and himself quickening it, he was, without inconsistency, quickening the universe as well, and was in every process of nature, and was outside the whole, and while known from the body by his works, he was none the less manifest from the working of the universe as well.[26]

There is a slightly different way to think about the abstract-nature view.[27] Consider the possibility that there are not different kinds of soul as the Alvinized version assumes. The Alvinized version states that the Word became a human soul at the Incarnation. So, presumably, there are such things as human souls, and another soul-like entity that is the divine nature, and perhaps other kinds of souls too, such as angelic souls that are different from either the divine nature or human souls. But perhaps there are not kinds of souls as there are natural kinds. Perhaps there are only souls *simpliciter*. In this way,

---

[26] Athanasius, *On the Incarnation of the Word*, trans. A. Robertson, in Edward R. Hardy (ed.), *Christology of the Later Fathers* (Philadelphia: Westminster Press, 1954), pp. 70–71. This is one patristic expression of the so-called *extra calvinisticum*.

[27] In fact, given the taxonomy of views outlined earlier, there may well be several others. But this view is pertinent to the current discussion. It might be thought that this second view is merely a clarification of the Alvinized view. But I think it could also serve as a distinct argument for substantially the same conclusion about the human nature of Christ.

---

other without supplying a good reason for doing so (such as, that one contradicts Scripture while the other does not). And in any case, even if a person did take the monothelite view, it would be incumbent upon him or her to show how monothelitism does not contradict the spirit – not just the letter – of Chalcedonian Christology (viz. one person in two distinct natures), since the received wisdom of the vast majority of the tradition, following the Fathers of the Third Council of Constantinople, such as Maximus, has been in favour of the dyothelite position.

But, whatever one makes of two-part Christologies that are monothelite (or appear monothelite), it seems to me that there is a strong case for retaining dyothelitism. There is biblical support for the doctrine (e.g. 'not my will, but your will be done' Luke 22:42[22]); it is, as we have already seen, affirmed by one of the (later) ecumenical councils of the Church and by almost all orthodox theologians;[23] and (I would argue) it is difficult to see how Christ could be said to be fully human without having a human will that is distinct from the divine will.[24]

---

[22] That is, this and other biblical passages have traditionally been thought to support dyothelitism (although some might not think this passage does support this doctrine). Compare St Maximus the Confessor's *Opusculum 6*: 'It follows then, that having become like us for our sake, he was willing to call on his God and Father in a human manner (*anthropoprepôs*) when he said, *Let not what I will, but what you will prevail*, inasmuch as, being God by nature, he also in his humanity has, as his human volition, the fulfilment of the will of the Father.' From *On the Cosmic Mystery of Jesus Christ*, trans. Paul M. Blowers and Robert Louis Wilken (Crestwood: St Vladimir's Seminary Press, 2003), p. 176.

[23] The Orthodox accept the first seven general councils of the Church as normative for doctrine; Roman Catholics accept many more conciliar statements than this. Protestant communions have typically affirmed the findings of the first four councils. Almost all orthodox Protestant theologians have affirmed dyothelitism (Augustus Strong is one exception). There are those communions that are monophysite (one-nature-ites), including the Syrian Church in India, the Coptic Church in Egypt, the Armenian Church and the Ethiopian Church. These churches reject the Chalcedonian settlement and dyothelitism.

[24] Pannenberg hints that the dyothelite settlement after Constantinople in AD 681 was at least partially due to political factors (which is true, but irrelevant to the truth or

Two abstract-nature views: Apollinarianism and monothelitism

We come to the question of the orthodoxy of the abstract- and concrete-nature views, beginning with the former. There are at least two ways in which the abstract-nature view can avoid Apollinarianism. (At least, I can think of two without much effort. I would not want to deprive ingenious theologians of the pleasure of thinking of others, particularly versions of this view that yield a three-part Christology.) The first of these is inspired by Alvin Plantinga's article 'On heresy, mind, and truth'. I shall dub this the *Alvinized abstract-nature view*.

In assuming the property or properties of human nature at the Incarnation, the Word assumes the property of being a human soul. That is, at the virginal conception of Christ, when the Word assumes human nature, the Word becomes a human soul. In assuming human nature he assumes whatever property or properties are necessary and sufficient for the Word to become the human soul that exists in the body of Christ. However, this does not mean that the Word *replaces an existing human soul*. Instead, the Word becomes the soul of the body of Christ. And it is not that the Word stands in for a human soul because Christ has no human soul. Were this the case, this sort of abstract-nature view would be straightforwardly Apollinarian. Recall that, for our purposes, the problem with Apollinarianism is that it states that Christ has no human soul. Instead, he is indwelt and energized, so to speak, by the Word, standing in the place of a human soul. Thus Apollinarius could write: 'he [Christ] is not man though like man; for he is not consubstantial with man in the most important

falsity of what the Third Council of Constantinople canonized). He also remarks that the victory of the dyothelite position meant that 'the perception of the concrete vital unity of Jesus was basically lost'. Pannenberg is not alone in alleging that dyothelitism has this shortcoming. But, as we shall see, I think there is no reason why this must be the case for all Christologies that are dyothelite. See Pannenberg, *Jesus – God and Man*, p. 294.

element [viz. a soul].' In fact, as Charles Raven [narius' thinking in this matter is summed up in th dwelling in man is not man; spirit united to flesh man as has been said titularly, for He is divine spirit u The problem with this is that it means that Christ is n because he lacks one essential property of being human ing a human soul. So, Apollinarianism cannot meet the for orthodox Christology laid out by the Council of Ch

The Alvinized version of the abstract-nature view is n forwardly Apollinarian, because it states that at the Incar Word *becomes a human soul*. This is possible because at nation the Word takes on the property of being a human s with all the other properties or conjuncts of the property nature'. Compare the strange case of Professor Magus Morph Morphelupus is a young scientist of the mad variety. He dev procedure that will transform him into a werewolf, knowing he willingly undergoes this procedure he will take on the pro or properties of being a werewolf. Naturally, being a mad scien Morphelupus undergoes this procedure and is transformed. Par the process of transformation involves Morphelupus's mind bei changed into the mind of a wolf, for the duration of the experimen until the effects of the procedure wear off (after a few days, say Thereupon, he returns to his (human) senses.

This is a limited analogy to the Alvinized version of the abstract-nature view. The point I am trying to make is that Morphelupus is fully wolf immediately after the procedure, and this means that his mind becomes the mind of a wolf. (I am not making any further claims for the analogy between Morphelupus and the Incarnation.) In a similar way, on the Alvinized view, the Word becomes a human soul at the Incarnation because the Word takes on the property of being a human soul belonging to the human body of Christ. This does not mean that the Word ceases to be a divine person. Nor does

[25] Cited in Charles Raven, *Apollinarianism*, p. 188.

souls are unlike material things, which can be classified according to natural kinds. There is the kind *dog*, the kind *horse*, and the kind *human*. All of these are kinds of material thing (although not all of them are just material things, if there are such thing as souls). But perhaps there are no distinctions like the distinction of natural kinds among souls. Souls are not classifiable into different kinds of soul in the same way that material bodies are classifiable in different natural kinds, such as horses and humans. Perhaps there is just the supernatural kind, soul.[28]

What would it mean for a particular body to have a soul on this view? It would mean only that a particular soul is conjoined with a particular body. Or, perhaps, it would mean that a particular soul is conjoined with a particular body for the period of the life of that particular body. Assume, for the sake of the argument, that a body is conceived and that at that moment of conception a particular soul is conjoined to this bundle of cells from thenceforth until the death of the particular body. Then, for that period, the soul in question is the soul of this particular body. We could refer to it in a rather colloquial way as 'this human soul' or, perhaps better, 'the soul attached to this human body'. But, in fact, all that is required for a soul to become the soul of a particular body is that a soul is conjoined with that body for the period the body is alive (from conception to expiration, say). There is no sense in which, strictly speaking, there are souls that are 'human souls', although we may classify them as such. There are just souls who have been selected by God to be attached to this particular body for a particular period of time. (This story implies a Platonic view of the relation between souls and bodies. But a hylomorphic view could be substituted for this one without destroying the point I am trying to make. One obvious difference on a hylomorphic account is that the soul joined to a particular body

---

[28] I mean that, possibly, souls do not form one kind (of thing), not that there is not more than one kind of soul. I take it that orthodox Christians do not want to affirm that there is only one soul in which different living things participate (in some fashion).

would provide the form for the matter of the body. But conceivably, a different soul could organize the same matter. Perhaps that organization would be slightly different. If that is right, then perhaps God selects the soul + body combination he does in order that a certain sort of material organization take place in this particular person.)

If we take this approach to the abstract-nature view, then it is clear that the divine soul of the second person of the Trinity could be conjoined with a particular human body in the Incarnation and, *by that very act*, be constituted a 'human soul' (in our colloquial sense of that phrase). For if there are no human souls as such, just souls attached to this particular body for this particular period of time, then all that is required for a soul to be counted as a 'human soul' is for that soul to be in a certain relationship of attachment to a certain body for a certain period during which the body in question is alive.

Call this version of the abstract nature view the *Reaified abstract-nature view*, in honour of Professor Michael Rea, who first suggested this to me. Like the Alvinized version, this offers a second abstract-nature construal of the Incarnation that does not entail Apollinarianism. On the Reaified version, the Word assumes the property or properties requisite for human nature, and one of those properties is that of being in a certain relation of attachment to this particular parcel of matter that is the human flesh of Jesus of Nazareth. In virtue of this relation, the Word becomes the soul attached to this body for the period of the life of this body. And in so doing, he becomes a 'human soul'. Essentially, he is not a kind of soul, a human soul, because there are no such things as *human* souls; there are just souls.[29] However, for the theological purpose of making sense of the Incarnation (and in a loose and non-philosophical way), we could say that the Word becomes a human soul. The important point to note here is that a

---

[29] Does this view obfuscate the Creator–creature distinction? What differentiates the divine nature from a created soul? For one thing, they have different properties. Aside from the fact that the divine nature has properties, like 'being omnipotent' and 'being omniscient', that created souls do not, the divine nature also has the property 'being uncreated', whereas all creaturely souls have the property 'being created'.

'human soul' does not distinguish a certain sort of soul distinct from, say, angelic souls (which is the more conventional way to think about souls). Thus, the Reified version of the abstract-nature view can be expressed in a way that, like the Alvinized version, avoids Apollinarianism. We can speak with the vulgar and say that the Word becomes a human soul. But we can think with the learned, that this actually means that the Word is attached to this particular parcel of matter, that is, this body, for the period of Incarnation, and that this is all that is required for the Word to be the soul of this particular human body.

However, problems lurk in the neighbourhood of this Reified view, aside from the obvious fact that the Reified view depends on a controversial claim about the nature of souls. The first of these (not directly related to the question in hand) is: Can any old soul be attached to a body and become a human soul in this sense? The answer to this question depends, in part, on which creatures are thought to have souls. If, following in the footsteps of Descartes, we say that animals other than humans, like horses and dogs, are soulless, then the answer to this question would appear to be affirmative. Any old soul *can* be attached to a human body and become a human soul in the relevant sense. On such a view, souls that are known to human beings as angels can become attached to certain parcels of matter. Indeed, from passages like Genesis 19, Isaiah 6 and Luke 2, it seems that there are angels who seem to be 'enfleshed' in this way. (I say *seem* because it may be that the angels in the Bible who appear to human beings only appear to have physical form. They may be able, through some occult means, to simulate human form. Or they may, like ghosts, be able to assume some 'subtle matter' that has peculiar properties such as being able to be perceived as physical and being able to pass through walls or fly or disappear at will, and so on.[30]) So, this view can take account of the fact that some souls

---

[30] For more on the subtle matter of souls, see Joshua Hoffman and Gary S. Rosenkrantz, *The Divine Attributes* (Oxford: Blackwell, 2002), ch. 3. For an interesting biblical case, see Acts 12.7.

are enfleshed and counted as 'human', and others are not and are counted (by humans at least) as angelic or demonic, or whatever.[31] This is not to lapse into language of kinds of souls. I am merely suggesting, on this view, that these different souls may be counted as different in kind by those who do not know any better, when in fact the only difference that is important for our purposes (apart from the different and individuating properties different and individual souls have – whatever they may be) is that this soul is enfleshed and counted as a human soul, while another soul is not.[32] However, the concession to a Cartesian view of animals other than humans as soulless automata may well be too high a price for many sympathetic to this way of cashing out the Reified version of an abstract-nature view of Christ's humanity.

Matters are worse for the Reified view if it is thought that animals other than humans have souls. Then it looks as though a soul attached to a cat, or a dog, could just as easily be attached to a human. But this generates the following *reductio ad absurdum*: If any soul can be attached to any body, and many kinds of animals, other than humans, have souls, then we could really have cases where frogs, or the souls attached to frogs, become princes, or souls attached to princes. We might, in deference to the Brothers Grimm, call this the *frog-prince problem* for the Reified view. God could change the

---

[31] Famously, Thomas declared that every angelic soul is its own 'kind', whereas human souls are instances of a natural kind because of their ability to procreate. But I am not concerned with that here. See *Summa Theologiae* 1.50.4.

[32] There is another problem here, similar to this one: Can one soul be attached to a body from t1 to t2, only to be substituted for another soul, attached to the same body, from t3 to t4? This need not be a problem if what we have here is two persons in one body, not one person with two different souls, assuming that souls are persons who are contingently attached to bodies. If they are not Cartesian souls but hylomorphic souls, then we do not seem to have the same person either, although for slightly different reasons. The form given to the matter of the body changes at t3 when it is organized by the second soul. In any case, this is not a problem confined to the Reified version of the abstract-nature view. It is common to any theory of personal identity through time that assumes substance dualism.

material organization of the body concerned from frog to prince, and retain the same soul. But this seems absurd.

A second problem has to do with the relationship between the Reified view and the *imago Dei* (image of God) in human beings. If it is thought that the *imago Dei* attaches to the souls of human beings, as properties of those souls, then it looks as though there are kinds of souls after all. Or at least, there is a kind of soul that is human, because only those souls with the property of the *imago Dei* will be able to act as souls for human bodies. If this were true, a soul without this property, such as the soul of an angel (or a frog), would not be able to be attached to a human body to form a human being. And, it need hardly be said, this is the traditional way in which the doctrine of the image of God in man has been understood.[33]

The third problem with this view is theological, and applies to all abstract-nature views. Although the Alvinized and Reified versions of the abstract-nature view may avoid falling foul of Apollinarianism, they end up denying dyothelitism, the view that Christ had two wills, one human and the other divine. We can see this in the following:

(1) At the Incarnation the Word assumes (a complete) human nature.

This means that:

(2) at the Incarnation the Word assumes the property 'having a human body', and

---

[33] See, for example, McGuckin, who says of the Greek Fathers that 'the image of God was referred specifically to man, and concretely located in the soul (a common theme among the Greeks who also saw the image to be especially located in the nous or logos of humanity'. *The Westminster Handbook to Patristic Theology*, p. 179. The same is true of later theology. For instance, Wolfhart Pannenberg states: 'The classical understanding of the divine likeness in Christian theology relates it to the soul . . . Latin Scholasticism gave particular emphasis to the fact that the likeness lies primarily in the soul, and this came to be presupposed in Reformation and post-Reformation theology.' However, he is quick to remark that 'this understanding does not accord with what Gen. 1.26f. actually says'. *Systematic Theology*, II, pp. 206–207.

(3) at the Incarnation the Word assumes the property 'being a human soul'.

So far, these premises are common to abstract- and concrete-nature views. We have already seen that, given an abstract-nature view:

(4) the assumption of a human soul can be understood in at least two ways:

    (a) in addition to having a divine nature, the Word becomes a human soul by assuming the property of human nature (Alvinized view), or

    (b) the Word stands in a certain relation to the body of Christ assumed at the Incarnation which makes the Word the soul of the body of Christ (Reified view).

Now, it is theologically orthodox to affirm that:

(5) the Word is a divine person; hence, the Word has a will, and
(6) Christ is a human being; hence, Christ has a will.[34]

From the combination of (5) and (6) and one of the conjuncts of (4), it seems clear that the will of Christ is identical with the will of the Word. (I am presuming that the will of a person is not separable from the person. The will of a person cannot exist independently of the person whose will it is, so to speak.) Thus:

(7) the will of Christ just is the will of the person of the Word, and
(8) there is only one will in the theanthropic person of Christ.

Which is monothelitism. So, from the foregoing, it is clear that the Reified abstract-nature view is monothelitic. At the Incarnation the

---

[34] In the previous chapter, I made the point that Christ is a divine person with a human nature, not a human person possessed by the Word (which is Nestorianism). Here I claim that Christ is a human being. On my understanding of the metaphysics of the Incarnation, Christ is a human being because he has the relevant body–soul composite to be human. But he is not a human person because this body–soul composite is assumed by the Word at the Incarnation, before, as it were, it may become a person independent of the Word. I shall return to this point later in the chapter.

Word is the soul attached to the body of Christ. The will of Christ just is the will of the Word. There is no distinction between the two. The Alvinized view is also monothelitic. At the Incarnation the Word assumes the property of being a human soul in addition to being a divine soul. And the Word assumes the property of having a human will in the same way too. But this is a property of the Word. There is no room for there to be more than one will here. The will of Christ is a property of the Word. However, and importantly, this argument shows that the abstract-nature view is not Apollinarian, because, according to the two versions of the view we have been considering, Christ has either a human soul (Alvinized view), or a 'human' soul (Reified view). Thus a defender of one of these two versions of an abstract-nature view of the Incarnation, though committed to monothelitism, is not committed to Apollinarianism. Christ could have a human or a 'human' soul, and only one will.

Nevertheless, this is a serious problem with these two versions of an abstract-nature view. Possession of a will is constitutive of being either a human or a divine entity. So, if Christ is fully human he must have a distinct human will. And if he is fully divine he must have a distinct divine will. Yet on these two abstract-nature views, it seems that Christ has only a distinct divine will. In which case, Christ is not fully human. However, a defender of the abstract-nature view might dispute this. For instance, Plantinga asks:

> Shall we say that duothelitism is the idea that the will of Christ had both the nature of a human will and the nature of a divine will, in the abstract sense of 'nature'? The partisans of the abstract nature view would happily accept that. Or shall we say that duothelitism is the idea that there are two distinct concrete wills (supposing that in fact a will is a concrete object of some kind)? The concretists would happily accept *that*, and then it looks as if it's the abstractists that are tugging the laboring oar.[35]

---

[35] Plantinga, 'On heresy, mind, and truth', p. 185.

But this is not sufficient to avoid monothelitism, as we have con-strued it. We can, given Plantinga's comments, predicate two distinct properties of the Word Incarnate, namely 'having the nature of a human will' and 'having the nature of a divine will'. But this seems to mean that one subject, the Word, has a human will *qua* human soul of Christ, and a divine will *qua* divine soul of the Word. Possession of such a reduplicative property is hardly sufficient to demonstrate that the Word has *two distinct* wills. For Christ to be a fully human person he must have a will that is distinct from the divine will of the Word. But this is just what the defender of an Alvinized abstract-nature view cannot affirm.

It is rather like saying that Clark Kent, the mild-mannered newspa-per reporter, has one will *qua* Kent, while Superman has another *qua* Superman. What we mean here is that Superman-Clark Kent is one individual, with one will under two aspects: his will as superhero and his will as mild-mannered reporter. Similarly, what Plantinga seems to be saying is that the one Word is a person with a will that, in the Incarnation, has two aspects: the nature of a human will and the nature of a divine will. But if one affirms that humans have distinct wills, and that Christ is a fully human person, is it really sufficient to claim that this just means that the Word who inhabits the body of Christ wills certain things, and, as the eternal Word, wills other things? (We could say just that, to be fully human, one would have to have a complete, distinct human will. Having the 'nature of a human will' is not sufficient if this means 'having a human will *qua* divine Word'.) Yet this is what Plantinga seems to be offering as a way of construing the dyothelite claim on an abstract-nature view.

From this examination of two versions of the abstract-nature view, several things are clear. First, an abstract-nature view need not entail Apollinarianism. Second, these two versions of an abstract-nature view are consistent with the letter of the Chalcedonian defini-tion. However, this will not satisfy those who think dyothelitism is a natural development of Chalcedonian Christology. And this includes Roman Catholicism, the Orthodox and the vast majority of classical Protestant theologians.[36] Of course, these two views do not exhaust the possible ways in which an abstract-nature view could be expressed. Both the Alvinized and Reaified views are consistent with a two-part Christology. But, as we have already noted, an abstract-nature view is also compatible with a three-part Christology. Perhaps an advocate of both an abstract-nature view and a three-part Christology could make a case for dyothelitism too. Then, providing such a putative view were orthodox in other respects, there would be no impediment to maintaining both an abstract-nature view of a certain sort and dyothelitism. But this does not apply to either the Alvinized or Reaified versions of an abstract-nature view.

The concrete-nature view: Nestorianism and dyothelitism

We have already noted that the concrete-nature view does not entail Nestorianism. In other words, it does not entail that, (a) at the Incarnation, the Word assumes an already existing human being, and (b) the hypostatic union brought about by the Incarnation is a union of two distinct persons.

---

[36] We have already noted the declaration of the Third Council of Constantinople (AD 680–681) – the Sixth Ecumenical Council of the Church. This is affirmed by Roman Catholics, Orthodox and, according to some leading classical Protestant theologians like Charles Hodge, Protestants too (see *Systematic Theology*, II, pp. 404–405, where he defends dyothelitism). In any case, it is certainly true that almost all classical Protestant theologians agreed that Christ had two wills. See, e.g., Calvin, *Commentary on a Harmony of the Evangelists, Matthew, Mark and Luke* (Edinburgh: Calvin Translation Society, 1845), p. 233; Francis Turretin, *Institutes of Elenctic Theology*, II, trans. George Musgrave Giger, ed. James T. Dennison Jr (Phillipsburg, P&R Publishing Co., 1992), 13.7.14; W. G. T. Shedd, *Dogmatic Theology*, 3rd edn (Phillipsburg: P&R Publishing Co., 2003 [1889–1894]) p. 657. This is also true of Lutheran theology; see Francis Pieper, *Christian Dogmatics*, II (St Louis: Concordia, 1951), p. 65. For a dissenting voice, see the Baptist theologian Augustus Strong: 'Christ has not two consciousnesses and two wills, but a single consciousness and a single will.' *Systematic Theology*, single-vol. edn (New Jersey: Fleming H. Ravell, 1907), p. 695.

A variant of the first part of Nestorianism is the idea that the Word could assume an existing concrete particular, say, a human zygote, or a fertilized human egg, which does not as yet constitute a human person. Assume that there is some period, after fertilization, during which the cells that will develop into a human person are not attached to a soul. At this stage of development, these human cells are just a clump of matter. Now, at some moment after fertilization, at time t3, a soul is attached to this clump of matter. It is possible that the Word assumes this clump of matter at time t2, during the temporal window between fertilization and ensoulment, rather than at t3, the moment at which the fertilized egg, or the zygote, is ensouled. Then, at t2 the Word assumes a clump of matter that is not a human being immediately before it becomes a human being in virtue of ensoulment. But this means that the Word assumes an existing concrete particular, although not an already existing complete human being. This is not, strictly speaking, Nestorian. But it requires a two-stage Incarnation (involving a material body, and then the addition of a distinct, human soul), which seems peculiar and is certainly not a traditional view – in fact, it is a temporary or limited case of Apollinarianism.[37] In any case, an advocate of a concrete-nature view need not maintain that the Word assumes an existing human being or an existing clump of matter that has the potential to become a human being, or, indeed, that the Word assumes a human being whose material part pre-exists this assumption.

This leaves dyothelitism. It might be said that on the dyothelite view Christ is two *persons*, since if a will is constitutive of personhood, and Christ has two wills (indeed, according to the Sixth Ecumenical Council, two centres of action), then he seems to be two persons, one human and one divine. And this is a species of Nestorianism.

[37] Recall that Apollinarianism states that Christ has a human body but no 'rational' human soul, its place being taken by the Word. In this case, the Word assumes a human body at the conception of Christ but this body does not have a soul until some later stage of foetal development. But then, for some period between conception and ensoulment, the Word is joined with a mere human body.

William Lane Craig and J. P. Moreland, while not affirming that dyothelitism is Nestorian, nevertheless maintain that 'it is extraordinarily difficult to preserve the unity of Christ's person once distinct wills are ascribed to the Logos and to the individual human nature of Christ'.[38]

It seems to me that it is difficult to make sense of the human nature of Christ whichever position one opts for, and at least dyothelitism has the advantage of being the view endorsed by an ecumenical council of the catholic Church. (Even if this is not a knock-down, drag-out argument against the alternative view, the testimony of the Christian tradition should not be taken lightly in matters touching central and defining Christian dogma.) In any case, dyothelitism does not entail Nestorianism. The Chalcedonian theologians present at the Council of Constantinople in AD 680–681 would have spotted this if it did, and refrained from drafting a document in support of dyothelitism (particularly with Maximus present). And it is not difficult to see why they would have rejected any supposed entailment between dyothelitism and Nestorianism. All dyothelitism claims is that if Christ is fully human, he must have a human will that is distinct from the divine will.[39] To deny this is to deny the full humanity of Christ. This is not Nestorian, because it is not sufficient for Nestorianism. In order to distil Nestorianism from dyothelitism one would have to show that having the constituents of a complete human nature – including having a human will distinct from the divine will – is sufficient for Christ to be a complete human person apart from the person of the Word. But these constituents are not sufficient for this task. To explain why, consider the following two arguments that draw upon Brian Leftow's presentation of these matters in 'A timeless God Incarnate'.

---

[38] *Philosophical Foundations for a Christian Worldview*, p. 611.

[39] For instance, Christ's two wills may be two centres of action for one person (which seems akin to the substance, though not the language, of Maximus' views on the subject).

The first involves the claim that every human zygote has the property 'constituting a distinct, individual human person when composed of a body + distinct soul, intellect and will, *unless assumed by a divine person*'. Perhaps, Leftow suggests, God 'built a slot for his incarnation into human nature. If one is willing to jigger [*sic*] with human nature in this way, one can allow that every other zygote on its own composes or constitutes a human being, but the zygote [of Christ] did not.'[40] This seems possible, even if, to some readers, it seems somewhat strange. Such a view entails dyothelitism, but is not Nestorian. The human nature assumed by the Word does have a distinct will; it is truly human. But it is not a person independent of the Word, because (a) it is assumed at the moment of its creation and, thus, at no time constitutes a person without the Word, and (b) in virtue of being assumed by the Word, it is incapable of becoming an individual without the Word, because it bears the property 'constituting a distinct, individual human person when composed of a body + distinct soul, intellect and will, *unless assumed by a divine person*'. Moreover, it seems to me that although a human being could be created by the miraculous work of the Holy Spirit in the womb of Mary, the product of such divine activity *sans* Incarnation would not constitute the person of Christ, although it would constitute a human person.

But perhaps this is a little too much for some to swallow. Alternatively, if a human body–soul composite usually comprises an individual human person, in the case of the Incarnation the body and soul of Christ are conjoined with the soul of the Word to form a 'larger' person.[41] Assume that at time t_1 Christ is composed of a

---

[40] 'A timeless God Incarnate', p. 281. Two comments: it is not clear to me why this need involve 'jiggering' of the kind Leftow implies. And, it might be that this property is unique, not to human beings, but to created natures *per se*, or to certain sorts of created natures, if one believes that God could be incarnated in something other than a human being.

[41] See Leftow, 'A timeless God Incarnate'. He uses Geach's famous '1001 cats' paradox to make the same point.

human body, a human soul (distinct from the soul of the Word) and the Word. Is it the case that, say, the human body and soul of Christ without the Word are a proper part of this composite object that is the person of Christ? Not necessarily. Although, normally, a human body and soul when conjoined do compose a human person, in the case of Christ, they do not, because they are assumed by the Word to compose a 'larger' person, hypostatically united in the Incarnation. Remove one component of this 'larger' person, the Word, say, or some combination of at most two of the components of this version of a concrete-nature view, and what is left is not the person of Christ, but some other thing. Perhaps, if the components are the human body and human soul that would have made up the 'larger' person of Christ, what remains is some other human being. But even if this is the case, this human being is not the person of Christ. The principle at work here is that, given a set of parts composing a concrete particular that is an instance of a natural kind at a particular time, no subset of that set of parts composes a member of the same kind at the same time. Once again, this seems to imply dyothelitism if the human nature involved is truly human. But it is not Nestorian.[42]

But it might be thought that the 'larger' person composed by the Incarnation does not, perhaps, constitute an instance of a natural (or supernatural) kind. Even if we grant this, it could be that this sort of principle is analogous to what is involved in the Incarnation. In some 'stretched' or extended sense, it could be said that the parts making up the person of Christ are such that no collection of those parts less than the total number of parts composes another thing of

---

[42] There are well-known counter-examples to this sort of argument. For instance, if three crowns are made into a triple tiara (such as the Pope wears), are the three crowns destroyed in this process? If one thinks not, then it looks as if one has a whole made up of three proper parts, each of which is a member of the same kind, 'crown'. But this analogy is only partial. The three crowns were all members of the same kind prior to the assembly of the triple tiara. The various 'parts' of Christ, on this version of a three-part Christology, are not clearly instances of the same kind prior to their 'assembly'.

the same sort as the parts that together make up the person of Christ. This sort of incarnational mereological sum seems plausible, and is orthodox. Take away the Word and, assuming the remaining parts of the person of Christ can form a human being, the product of such a union is not the person of Christ, even if the person thus formed is born to the Virgin Mary, is called Jesus and lives in Nazareth.[43] For without the hypostatic union with the Word, what we have is not Christ, the God-Man. What we have is just a man. In fact, what we seem to have is a different man, someone who is not God Incarnate. But none of this means that an advocate of a concrete-nature view is committed to Nestorianism just because they are committed to dyothelitism. So it seems that there are (at least) two ways in which advocates of a concrete-nature view can argue that dyothelitism need not entail Nestorianism.

Two final thoughts

In this chapter, I have left out discussion of two things to which I will now briefly refer. Richard Swinburne raises the first. He says that much of the confusion about the relation between the natures and person of Christ stems from a failure to clarify what is meant by the human soul of Christ. If one takes a rather Platonic view of the body–soul composite, the result looks Nestorian because on this way of thinking the soul is separate from and only contingently related to

---

[43] There may be an application of mereological essentialism here. For present purposes, this is the thesis that a particular composite object cannot have any other parts than it does, and a loss of any of these parts would mean the destruction of the object concerned. This means that the 'larger' person of Christ cannot be composed of some number of parts less than the number it does have: say, the human body and soul of Christ without the Word. This would not be the person of Christ. However, this need not mean that the Word could not have assumed some other concrete particular. It just means that, once the Word has assumed a concrete particular in Incarnation, the mereological sum of this concrete particular + the Word existing in hypostatic union is essential for the persistence of that object.

the matter of the body. On the hylomorphic account the soul gives the matter of the body the form it enjoys (in fact, it *is* the form it enjoys). Although this is a contingent relation – this soul need not be conjoined to this body – the relation between soul and body is much more intimate because it involves the 'organization' of the matter of the body by the soul. Swinburne thinks that this sounds much less Nestorian and that it is far more likely that the Fathers of Chalcedon had this sort of view in mind when thinking of the human soul and human body of Christ.[44]

This may be true. But, as I have already indicated, I think a hylomorphic account of the Incarnation can be given that has the same result as the version of the concrete-nature view + three-part Christology I have outlined. I have not defended this way of thinking about the Incarnation because I do not think the hylomorphic account is the best account of the relation between souls and bodies, even if the Fathers were thinking in these terms when they drafted the Chalcedonian definition. (I do not think the Chalcedonian definition precludes a Platonic understanding of the body–soul relation.) If the concrete-nature view given here is compatible with Chalcedon, that is sufficient for my purposes. If it turns out that the hylomorphic account is another coherent rendering of the Chalcedonian definition, then so much the better for the relevant versions of the concrete-nature view.

A second point has to do with the relationship between abstract- and concrete-nature views. Leftow says:

> To be a human being is surely to be a person 'owning' a human body, soul, mind and will. If this is right, then someone acquires the property of being human only if that person comes to 'own' the full human natural endowment: that is, abstract-nature incarnation takes place only if concrete-nature incarnation does. Equally, concrete nature incarnation takes place only if abstract-nature incarnation

44 See Swinburne, *The Christian God*, Additional Note 14, p. 252.

does: God has not done what he wanted to do by taking on a human natural endowment unless by doing so he comes to exemplify the property of being human. So one could not believe in abstract-nature incarnation without also believing in concrete, and vice-versa. But the symmetry ends there. One does not usually interact directly with properties, 'assuming' or 'exemplifying' them. Concrete things act, and in virtue of their activities, they come to exemplify properties. Abstract-nature incarnation can take place only *by* concrete-nature incarnation. In this sense, the concrete-nature view of the incarnation has to be basic.[45]

The real problem, according to Leftow, is between one- and two-mind theories of the Incarnation, or, as he puts it, two- or three-part theories of the Incarnation. This seems to me to be partially correct, given a hylomorphic account of the body–soul relationship. (And Leftow's central point about what it is to be a human person is true, *mutatis mutandis*, for a more Platonic or Cartesian account of the soul–body relationship as well.) But I think his remarks are only partially true, because what he says about the relation between concrete- and abstract-nature views is not quite right. For one thing, if a concrete-nature view *entails* an abstract-nature view and vice versa, then it is not clear on what basis one is more fundamental, or more basic, than the other. And if a concrete-nature view entails an abstract-nature view, then we are entitled to ask whether all concretists are monothelites, or whether all abstractists are dyothelites. This seems implausible. Better to retain, rather than attempt to collapse, the distinction we began with, between concrete- and abstract-nature views on the one hand, and two- and three-part Christologies on the other. As I maintained there, these two sorts of view do not entirely overlap. A theologian could affirm both an abstract-nature view and a three-part Christology, or a two-part Christology and a concrete-nature view (although this last may well be unorthodox). If

---

[45] Leftow, 'A timeless God Incarnate', p. 279, emphasis original.

this is right, then matters are rather more complicated than Leftow allows for (and I say this as someone who is in sympathy with the great majority of what Leftow so clearly and eloquently says on the metaphysics of the Incarnation). Nevertheless, he is right to point out the intimate relationship that exists between these two ways of characterizing the human nature of Christ, and the fact that characteristic contemporary accounts of abstract-nature views like Plantinga's do end up advocating a one-mind/two-part Christology. All of which raises the following question: Which is the right view of Christ's human nature? Which combination of these views gets at what the human nature of Christ really consists in? Much here depends on metaphysical intuitions that are difficult to fathom. The fact that there appear to be several different views on the human nature of Christ that have persisted in the Christian tradition only goes to show how deep-seated these intuitions are, and how difficult it is to show that one view is a more adequate account of the matter than the other.[46]

Conclusions

What I have attempted to provide in this chapter is some clarification of several different views of Christ's human nature that are theologically interesting. I have also attempted to sketch the ways in which different views of Christ's human nature and what one thinks about properties are interrelated. It is surprising how few modern

---

[46] Much here depends on the role of intuitions and how they inform theological (and metaphysical) reasoning. It seems to me that we reason and argue on the basis of intuitions that are immediate apprehensions of what a particular thing is. Moreover, in the case of things like the human nature of Christ, people often have deep-seated intuitions that are contrary to the similarly deep-seated intuitions of others on the same subject. This is not to deny that intuitions can change. But it seems to me that they are fundamental components of our thinking that are often difficult to alter, and on the basis of which we form arguments for particular conclusions.

theologians have attempted such an account before now.[47] Perhaps this is a partial explanation of the longstanding confusion over what the human nature of Christ actually is. It seems to me that the combination of a concrete-nature view and three-part Christology is to be preferred to the other options that have been considered, not because it is coherent and the alternatives are not, but because the other views are either unorthodox (e.g. two-part Christologies with a concrete-nature view that are Apollinarian) or monothelitic. The fact is that monothelitism was condemned by an ecumenical council of the Church. This makes it unorthodox too. Of course, if it is possible to construct an abstract-nature view coupled with a three-part Christology that is not monothelitic, then this is another option open to the theologian concerned to remain orthodox. I think that a good theological rule of thumb is this: if a doctrine contradicts the teaching of Scripture, it is automatically outside orthodox Christian belief. If a doctrine contradicts the implicit teaching of Scripture and the explicit declaration of an ecumenical council – such as the denial of the Trinity – this is also outside orthodox Christian belief. However, if a doctrine is not excluded by Scripture and can find support in the tradition, but contradicts the teaching of an ecumenical council, things are a little trickier. It seems to me that even here, one would have to show that the council in question endorsed some teaching that was itself contrary to Scripture – for what else can trump the authority of an ecumenical council of the Church, except Scripture? But the declaration of the Third Council of Constantinople in favour of dyothelitism is not obviously contrary to Scripture (I would argue that it is implied in several passages of Scripture) and does stand in the Chalcedonian tradition. There is even a good historical case that can be made for the view that the Third Council of Constantinople

---

[47] There are conspicuous exceptions from philosophical theologians interested in the medieval disputes, like Brian Leftow, Richard Cross, Thomas Flint, Marilyn Adams or Alfred Freddoso. But among contemporary *systematic* theologians, there are almost no such discussions.

was engaged in explicating Chalcedonian orthodoxy in an attempt to prevent monothelites from offering a compromise to monophysites unhappy with the Chalcedonian settlement, thereby vitiating what Chalcedon had achieved. So, why endorse Chalcedonian Christology and repudiate Constantinopolitan dyothelitism? The usual answer is that there are good metaphysical (rather than theological) reasons for rejecting dyothelitism, to do with whether or not having two wills entails Nestorianism. But dyothelitism does not entail Nestorianism. The two wills of Christ could be understood to be something like two theatres of action in one person, one *qua* human and one *qua* divine, but without the dysfunction in the human will brought about by the noetic effects of sin in other, fallen human beings. This is akin to the view expressed by Maximus the Confessor, whose Christology was instrumental in forging the decree of the Third Council of Constantinople, and falls short of Nestorianism. Like Maximus and the Fathers of the Third Council of Constantinople, I take it that if Christ had no distinct human will he was not fully human. And, like most of the Fathers and the medieval schoolmen, I take it that a human nature is not fundamentally a property, but a concrete particular composed of a human body and a distinct soul. For these reasons, I am drawn towards the combination of a concrete-nature view + three-part Christology, and away from versions of the abstract-nature view that deny one aspect or more of this position.

3 | The *anhypostasia–enhypostasia* distinction

For He took on Himself the elements of our compound nature, and these not as having an independent existence or as being originally an individual, and in this way assumed by Him, but as existing in His own subsistence.

St John of Damascus

In the theological literature the human nature of Christ is sometimes described as an *anhypostatos physis*, that is, a (human) nature that exists independently of an individual or *hypostasis*. This, it is said, is consistent with the idea that Christ's human nature does not exist as a *person* (*hypostasis*) independent of its assumption by the Word. Instead, the human nature of Christ is said to be 'impersonal' prior to the Incarnation and, from the first moment of Incarnation onwards, *enhypostatos*, that is, a (human) nature that exists 'in' a particular person or *hypostasis*.[1] One way of understanding this would be to say that the human nature assumed by the second person of the Trinity, though never a person as such (independent of the Word), exists 'in'

---

[1] See Donald Baillie, *God Was in Christ* (London: Faber and Faber, 1961), ch. 4; G. C. Berkouwer, *The Person of Christ* (Grand Rapids: Eerdmans, 1954), ch. 12; John Knox, *The Humanity and Divinity of Christ* (Cambridge: Cambridge University Press, 1967), ch. 4; Heinrich Heppe, *Reformed Dogmatics*, trans. G. T. Thompson (London: Wakeman Trust, 1950), ch. 17; Donald Macleod, *The Person of Christ* (Leicester: Inter-Varsity Press, 1998), ch. 7; Herbert M. Relton, *A Study in Christology: The Problem of the Relation of the Two Natures in the Person of Christ* (London: SPCK, 1917), passim; and Richard Swinburne, *The Christian God* (Oxford: Oxford University Press, 1994), pp. 213ff. The literature in this area is considerable. I have given only a few representative examples.

the *hypostasis* or person of the Word and is thereby 'personalized' (that is, *hypostatized*) by the Word. Sometimes this is articulated in terms of the human nature of Christ existing 'within', or being 'taken up into', the Word. Karl Barth is often cited as a champion of what we might call this *an–enhypostasia* distinction in recent theology. He says:

> *Anhypostasis* asserts the negative. Since in virtue of the *egeneto*, i.e., in virtue of the *assumptio*, Christ's human nature has its existence – the ancients said, its subsistence – in the existence of God, meaning in the mode of being (*hypostasis*, 'person') of the Word, it does not possess it in and for itself, *in abstracto*. Apart from the divine mode of being whose existence it acquires, it has none of its own; i.e., apart from its concrete existence in God in the event of the *unio*, it has no existence of its own, it is *anhypostatos*. *Enhypostatos* asserts the positive. In virtue of the *egeneto*, i.e., in virtue of the *assumptio*, the human nature acquires existence (subsistence) in the existence of God, meaning in the mode of being (*hypostasis*, 'person') of the Word. This divine mode of being gives it existence in the event of the *unio*, and in this way it has a concrete existence of its own, it is *enhypostatos*.[2]

---

[2] *Church Dogmatics*, 4 vol., trans. Geoffrey Bromiley and T. F. Torrance (Edinburgh: T. & T. Clark, 1936–1969), 1/2, p. 163. Barth claims he finds this distinction in the Protestant orthodox and that the orthodox, in turn, found the distinction in Leontius of Byzantium. This has been challenged by F. LeRon Schults in 'A dubious Christological formula: from Leontius of Byzantium to Karl Barth', *Theological Studies* 57 (1996), pp. 431–446. Schults claims that Barth mistakenly thinks that this formula can be found in Leontius of Byzantium, when in fact this is 'an invention of Protestant Scholasticism' (p. 431). However, Uwe M. Lang has defended Barth in 'Anhypostatos–enhypostatos: Church Fathers, Protestant orthodoxy and Karl Barth', *Journal of Theological Studies* n.s. 49 (1998), pp. 630–657. He concurs that the Leontius of Byzantium connection is false, but shows that the Protestant orthodox did derive the *anhypostatos–enhypostatos* distinction from one of the Church Fathers, John of Damascus. See also Ivor Davidson, 'Theologizing the human Jesus: an ancient (and modern) approach to Christology reassessed', *International Journal of Systematic Theology* 3 (2001), pp. 129–153.

This way of speaking about the *anhypostatos physis* and *enhypostatos physis* is, it seems to me, somewhat misleading, for it could be taken to mean that the two aspects of the *an–enhypostasia* distinction are negative and positive ways of stating the same thesis. But this is not the case. If it were, then it is not clear why some theologians have rejected one aspect of the distinction and retained the other (unless, of course, these theologians were just confused about what the an–enhypostatic nature of Christ's humanity is).[3] This rather ambiguous way of stating the distinction is repeated quite often, even when it is apparent that the author intends to convey some difference of meaning between the two aspects of the distinction (as it seems Barth does). Compare Ivor Davidson's recent characterization, which is a little clearer than Barth is on this point, while making a similar, and to my mind unhelpful, point about the *anhypostatos physis* (impersonal (human) nature) being the negative of the *enhypostatos physis* (personalized (human) nature):

> The heart of this *theologoumenon* [viz. the *an–enhypostasia* distinction] can be stated quite simply: the human nature of Jesus has no *hypostasis* of its own (it is '*anhypostatic*'), but subsists only and always as the human nature of the Son of God, the second person of the Trinity (it is thus '*enhypostatic*' in him. . . . Negatively, the humanity of Jesus has no independent reality of its own; positively, it is *hypostatized* in union with, or in (*en-hypostasis*), the person of the Logos.[4]

I cite these two examples simply to illustrate the fact that much ink has been spilt in the theological literature trying to explain how Christ has a human nature that is both anhypostatic and enhypostatic. Although

---

[3] H. R. Mackintosh epitomizes theologians unsympathetic to the concept of an *anhypostatos physis* (impersonal (human) nature): 'No real meaning could be attached to a human "nature" which is not simply one aspect of the concrete life of a human person.' *The Doctrine of the Person of Jesus Christ* (Edinburgh: T. & T. Clark, 1912), p. 207.

[4] Ivor Davidson, 'Theologizing the human Jesus', p. 135.

no ecumenical council has canonized this distinction, it has enjoyed considerable influence and, since the period of Protestant orthodoxy in the post-Reformation period, has become something of a touchstone for discussions of the human nature of Christ. Whether one agrees with this distinction as a whole or in part, rejects it in its entirety as hopelessly confused, or regards it as an unnecessary theological accretion, it has undoubtedly played an important role in making sense of the human nature of Christ in Christology. It therefore behoves us to take it seriously as something that is often thought to shed light on an important aspect of Christology.

The fact that this distinction has sometimes not been articulated as clearly as it might have been is largely because some theologians have not seen that it depends upon which view of the human nature of Christ one takes, and what one thinks about the relation between persons and natures in the hypostatic union. In this chapter we shall apply to the problem of the *an–enhypostasia* distinction what we gleaned by a consideration of this matter in the previous chapter. So, this is the sequel to the previous chapter, and much of what is discussed here depends on what was said there. I shall argue that this *an–enhypostasia* distinction makes most sense according to a concrete-nature view of the Incarnation, coupled with a three-part Christology.

Two abstract–nature accounts

We begin with those views of Christ's humanity that aver that human nature is a property that all human beings have essentially, and in particular a universal of which different human natures are instances. This, the reader will recall, is one sort of abstract-nature view (abstract because, on this view, human nature is a property and properties are abstract objects). Following Thomas Morris, let us call the composite property that makes up human nature the *kind essence* of human beings.[5] It might be that the kind essence of human beings is the property or property-set that all human beings share. But then, the human nature Christ has will be 'impersonal' in the sense that it is a property that is common to all human beings because it is a universal, like 'being a featherless biped' or 'being made in the image of God'. Call this version of the abstract-nature view of Christ's humanity the *realist view* of human natures.

If we follow this realist understanding of Christ's human nature, we might say that it is a universal – a kind essence – and argue that this alone is not sufficient for concrete human personhood. What is needed for concrete human personhood is for human nature to be exemplified by the person of the Word, in the hypostatic union. Only when the kind essence 'human being' is assumed by the Word can this kind essence be 'personalized', so to speak. Thus, if one thought the human nature of Christ was *fundamentally* a universal, it looks as though the *anhypostatos* aspect of the *an–enhypostasia* distinction is only trivially true; it says nothing about Christ that is peculiar to Christ. The Word assumes the property of human nature at the Incarnation. But, one might think, the same goes for any particular human being. All humans necessarily have the property of human nature from the first moment of their existence onwards. In which case, it seems strange that theologians would make a fuss of the fact that the human nature Christ possesses is *anhypostatic*. Surely, it is worth making a theological issue of this only if it expresses something particularly illuminating about the human nature of Christ. But if it is the case that all human beings have this kind essence, then all the *anhypostatos physis* means is that Christ, along with every other human being, shares the set of properties that are essential to being human, which are universals.

If this is right, then a defender of this realist view can affirm that an anhypostatic human nature does exist independently of the person

[5] Thomas V. Morris, *The Logic of God Incarnate* (Ithaca: Cornell University Press, 1986), ch. 2.

of Christ (it is, after all, a universal, or set of universals). This can be made clear by summing up what we have ascertained thus far. The human nature assumed by Christ is impersonal (the way the *anhypostatos* is often construed in the literature), because all human natures are impersonal in the sense that they are just kind essences, that is, abstract objects that are had by all instances of a particular natural kind. (So this is not something peculiar about the human nature of Christ and seems a rather unimportant point to make such theological mileage out of.) Nevertheless, the defender of a realist view could affirm that Christ's human nature was enhypostatic if this means nothing more than that the Word exemplifies human nature. Then an instance of human nature exists, as it were, 'in' the person of the Word. But notice that it is not that the human nature Christ exemplifies exists only because the Word possesses it in the Incarnation. If human nature is a kind essence, it exists as an abstract object irrespective of whether or not it is possessed by a person. So, on this understanding of Christ's human nature as an abstract object, it would be true, in a rather loose way, to say that the human nature of Christ is 'personalized' or 'hypostatized' by the Word in the Incarnation. But, once again, this does not seem to mean much more than the claim that a given entity is an instance of a particular kind (of thing). So, a particular entity will exemplify those properties that comprise the kind essence of the particular kind to which the entity belongs. We might want to express this in terms of the kind essence of human nature being 'hypostatized' in the Word. But this seems a little extravagant, when all it means is that the Word has these properties on becoming incarnate. But I suppose a defender of this view might want to claim that to this extent, or taken in this way, the *enhypostatos physis* makes sense (although it does seem to be a rather peculiar sense of *enhypostatos*, since it is difficult to see what it means to say that the human nature of Christ is hypostatized).

But what if it is thought that the human nature of Christ is a property or set of properties that is a *particular*, rather than a *universal*? In that case, as before, human nature may or may not be exemplified by

Christ, depending on whether or not the Word becomes incarnate. But the difference on this version of an abstract-nature view is that the human nature of Christ does not exist unless the person of Christ exists, because it does not exist as some universal independently of the person that possesses this universal. Or, to put it another way, on this way of thinking about the abstract-nature view, what we have is a commitment to one version of trope theory, according to which the human nature of Christ is a set of particulars that belong to Christ alone, and which cannot be possessed by some other object, because such objects do not exist apart from this particular object (as universals). But this trope version of an abstract-nature view means that human natures cannot exist independently of human persons. In which case, this version of the abstract-nature view is incompatible with the anhypostatic aspect of the *an–enhypostasia* distinction. For if the properties that comprise Christ's human nature cannot exist independently of Christ, as universals, then there can be no meaning to the notion of an *anhypostatos physis*. However, the trope view does make more sense of the enhypostatic aspect of the distinction. If Christ's human nature is a set of particulars rather than universals, it does make sense to say that the Word hypostatizes or personalizes these properties. Or, at least, it makes sense to say that the human nature of Christ exists only 'within' the person of the Word, who, in assuming these properties, hypostatizes them. So, it seems that there is a price to pay whichever of these two versions of an abstract-nature view one adopts. The realist version may make sense of the anhypostatic aspect, but at the cost of saying nothing that is not plainly an entailment of a realist theory of properties. And, although this view is compatible with one peculiar or gerrymandered way of thinking about the enhypostatic aspect of the *an–enhypostasia* distinction, it is so at the cost of appearing theologically insubstantial. One could opt for the trope account instead. This makes good sense of an *enhypostatos physis*, but no sense of an *anhypostatos physis*. This will only be a problem for theologians committed to both aspects of the distinction. As has already been pointed out, there are a number of theologians who find one or both aspects of the distinction unhelpful, or useless. For such theologians, this reasoning will hold no terror. But for theologians wanting to retain this distinction in its full strength, who think this makes an important theological point about the human nature of Christ, the two abstract-nature views we have discussed are not sufficient to the task (although, for different reasons.)[6] And of course, those who endorse a two-part Christology (Word + human body) will most naturally think in terms of human natures as abstract objects in this fashion.[7]

The concrete-nature account

Matters are somewhat different if we assume that human natures are concrete particulars, as those who defend a three-part Christology do. We might think of this view as including the following constituents:

(1) Human natures do not exist independently of human beings. (Human natures are concrete particulars.)
(2) Christ has a human nature in addition to a divine nature.

---

[6] It might be that what is important to a particular theologian is to make sense of Christ's human nature according to a particular metaphysical theory of properties and natures, such as contemporary essentialism (as, for example, with Alvin Plantinga's work, in *The Nature of Necessity* (Oxford: Oxford University Press, 1974)). Then one might be inclined towards the realist version of an abstract-nature view. Alternatively, like H. R. Mackintosh, Leontius of Byzantium and others, one might think that it just makes no sense to speak of an *anhypostatos physis*. In which case, one could happily embrace the trope nominalist theory and apply that to the human nature of Christ.

[7] What of those nominalists who are not trope theorists, but who believe that Christ's human nature is fundamentally a particular, or set of particulars, like the abstract-nature view? Applied to the *an–enhypostasia* problem the result would be similar to the trope view. That is, the *anhypostatos physis* would be meaningless (there are no properties at all). And the *enhypostatos physis* would be meaningful (Christ's human nature is just a particular, or a set of particulars, that is hypostatized by the Word in the Incarnation). The difference for the trope theorist has to do with the sort of particular this human nature is.

(3) The human nature of Christ exists because the Holy Spirit brings it into being.

(4) This human nature of Christ does not exist independently of the theanthropic person of Christ.

Here it is the case that human natures do not exist independently of human persons, because human natures are concrete particulars. And this is the case for all human natures, not just the human nature of Christ. What is assumed at the Incarnation, according to this view, is *a* particular human nature, not merely human nature *per se* (that is, taken as a universal). The concrete particular that is the human nature of Christ does not exist independently of the person of Christ. It becomes a human person on its assumption by the Word.

Furthermore, on this concrete-nature view, the only reason Christ's human nature exists is the virginal conception brought about by the Holy Spirit. Had the Holy Spirit not brought about the fertilization of the human egg in Mary's womb that became the human body of Christ, conjoined with the human soul that became Christ's human soul too, there would have been no human nature of Christ to speak of. The same is not true of other human beings[8] because most other human beings are brought into existence via a normal process of human procreation and gestation. But it is still the case for human beings besides Christ that their human natures exist simply because God brings it about that their bodies and souls (presuming that humans are made of body + soul) are joined in such a way that they become human beings. So, on what we might call the three-part concrete-nature view, unlike realist versions of the abstract-nature view, human natures do not exist independently of human beings, although Christ is a special case of this. In this respect, three-part concrete-nature views of Christ's humanity are similar to trope versions of the abstract-nature view.

[8] Except, perhaps, Adam and Eve, and, for some Christians, Mary *Theotokos.*

Indeed, this view is consistent with saying that human beings exemplify those properties requisite for being human in either a realist or a nominalist sense. It is just that, on the three-part concrete-nature view, having a human nature is not simply a matter of exemplifying certain properties, but possessing a certain sort of concrete particular (that has certain properties). In fact, on this three-part view, a human nature *is* a concrete particular that has certain properties. So, a defender of a concrete-nature view who is also a three-part Christologist could claim that Christ's human nature has those properties common to all human beings (a kind essence) as well as other properties that are particular to Christ's humanity, such as being born in Bethlehem in a manger, being in hypostatic union with the Word of God, and so forth. This is compatible with a realist understanding of properties. But it could be claimed that properties are just particulars, as with the trope, or other nominalist account. In which case, the properties of Christ's human nature are just particulars that only Christ could possess, in the same way that the properties of my human nature are just particulars that only I could possess. But, for the same reasons that would apply to the case of a two-part-Christology account of trope nominalism, I do not think trope nominalism can be used to defend the claim that Christ's human nature was anhypostatic. A three-part Christologist who wants to defend both aspects of the *an–enhypostasia* distinction needs to endorse some version of realism with respect to the properties the human nature of Christ possesses.

All of this raises the obvious question: How would a defender of the idea that human natures are concrete particulars, advocated by (among others) those who hold to a three-part Christology, make sense of the *an–enhypostasia* distinction? One way to do so would be as follows. On the question of an anhypostatic human nature, Christ has those properties that are common to all human beings (what we have previously called a kind essence). Assuming that the three-part Christologist wants to defend a full-blooded account of the *an–enhypostasia* distinction, she or he will opt for a realist, rather than a nominalist, understanding of the properties Christ's human nature possesses. Then, Christ has those properties that are necessary and sufficient for being human. And these properties exist independently of the Incarnation. So there is a real sense in which the three-part Christologist can affirm that Christ has a human nature that shares a core of properties with all other human beings, that exist independently of the particular human nature Christ possesses. However, the important difference between this concrete-nature view and, say, the realist version of an abstract-nature view is that, according to the former, it is not true to say merely that Christ has the properties that comprise some universal that is human nature. Rather, what we should say is that he has a human body and human soul distinct from the Word that form a concrete particular that is his human nature. But this concrete particular has certain properties that are held in common with other human beings, as well as those properties that are peculiar to Christ, such as being born to Mary in a Bethlehem stable in 4 BC.

It should be clear from this that, on a realist way of thinking about the concrete-nature view + three-part Christology combination, Christ's human nature is *enhypostatic*. That is, it exists only 'in' the person of the Word. This does not mean that Christ's human nature becomes a person on being assumed by the Word at the moment of Incarnation (the moment at which his human nature is also created). The human nature of Christ is not a person independent of the Word. Nor is the human nature of Christ a person in itself, as it were, once the Word has assumed it. It is the Word who is the personal subject of the Incarnation, and the Word who assumes this human nature (understood here as the natural endowment of a human being), literally 'personalizing' it in the process. So, the human nature of Christ is only ever the natural endowment of a person, even when assumed by the Word.[9] We could put it this way. The

---

[9] As Richard Swinburne has recently pointed out, Thomas claims that Christ is a person who is a human being, but is not a human person. Swinburne comments, 'I suppose

Word is fully a person 'prior' to the Incarnation. At the Incarnation he assumes the body–soul composite that is the natural endowment of a human being, which, in the case of other humans, would be sufficient to constitute a human person, but which does not do so in the case of Christ because the Word assumes it instead, thereby 'personalizing' it. Thus, it is the Word who is the logical subject of the body–soul composite that makes up his human nature. They are *his* human soul and body, and thereafter could not be the body and soul of any other person, because they have no existence independent of the Word from the first moment of the Incarnation onwards. The body–soul composite assumed by the Word is, as it were, 'bespoken', necessarily bespoken by and for the Word. So there never was a time at which the human nature of Christ existed independently of its assumption by the Word.[10]

If this can be sustained against counter-arguments, then three-part Christologists are able to account for the intuition (that is, the fundamental apprehension) behind the *an–enhypostasia* distinction that the human nature of Christ is 'impersonal' in one sense (Christ has those properties necessary and sufficient for being human, just as all human beings do), and 'personalized' or 'hypostatized' in that union (the human nature being a concrete particular that the Word assumes).[11]

that what this means is that Christ is not essentially human, while the rest of us are.' *The Christian God*, p. 214. Alfred J. Freddoso says much more about this in 'Human nature, potency and the Incarnation', *Faith and Philosophy* 3 (1986), pp. 27–53. But these are deep waters that we cannot wade into here.

[10] None of this contradicts the fact that, had the Word not assumed this human nature, it could have formed a human being who was not God Incarnate. I take it that there is a possible world in which this does take place. The point here is that *once it is assumed*, the human nature concerned is Christ's human nature. It cannot thereafter be the human nature of another.

[11] It might be thought, however, that each of the views as I have explained them has to gerrymander one of the aspects of the *an–enhypostasia* distinction in order to make sense of the whole. The realist version of an abstract-nature and two-part-Christology combination can affirm the *anhypostatos* without cavil, but has more difficulty

The assumption of human nature

It is also worth noting that there is no metaphysical possibility of the *theanthropic person* of Christ existing independently of the Incarnation. In other words, there is no possibility of the God-Man that is Jesus Christ existing independently of the Incarnation.[12] The Word is truly but only contingently a human being; he might not have become incarnate. And without an incarnation there would be no human nature that is assumed by the Word. This is the case irrespective of what one thinks human natures are. On the abstract-nature views we have discussed, the God-Man is a phase of the life of the Word simply because the Word assumes the property of human nature at the Incarnation (realist account) or certain particulars comprising Christ's human nature (trope account). And according to the concrete-nature views we are concerned with, the God-Man is a phase of the life of the Word simply because the Word assumes the human

---

making sense of the *enhypostatos*. (What does it mean to say Christ's human nature is personalized on this view, if it is a universal?) The trope version of an abstract-nature and two-part-Christology combination can affirm the *enhypostatos physis*, but is unable to make sense of the *anhypostatos physis*. But the three-part Christologist who thinks in terms of a concrete-nature view and realism has problems with the *anhypostatos*. (Is it sufficient to say Christ's human nature is impersonal just in terms of possessing all those properties shared common with other human beings?) Undoubtedly some will argue that none of these views can affirm both aspects of the whole *an–enhypostasia* distinction (which is what we set out to do). This may turn out to be the case. In which case, what is the *an–enhypostasia* distinction worth? But it seems to me that the three-part Christologist + concrete-nature defender who is a realist is able to hold on to the intuition behind the *anhypostasia* aspect of the distinction (if not the way in which this is often cashed out). So perhaps both aspects of the *an–enhypostasia* distinction can be retained, although one aspect, the *anhypostasia*, needs to be expressed more carefully in order to do so.

[12] The Word may have assumed another human nature – perhaps even another nature that was not human. Occam mooted this in his *asinus* Christology, which stated that the Word could have been incarnate as an ass (see Heiko Oberman, *The Harvest of Medieval Theology*, 3rd edn (Grand Rapids: Baker, 2000 [1963]), pp. 25off.). But that is another matter. The point here is to do with Christ in particular, not the possibility of incarnation as a general metaphysical thesis about the divine nature.

body and human soul of Christ, where the human soul is understood as distinct from the divine nature of the Word.[13] But without this assumption by the Word, there would be no theanthropic person of Christ, because the human body + (distinct) human soul that Christ has are not sufficient for the God-Man to exist. In this respect, the three-part view of the Incarnation (taken together with the view that natures are concrete particulars) means that Christ's humanity is unique. Whereas, in the case of other human beings, a body–soul composite is sufficient for the existence of a human person, this is not the case in the Incarnation. What is needed in addition to this in the case of Christ is the assumption of this concrete particular by the Word.[14]

But, it might be asked, is the Incarnation metaphysically necessary for the existence of the person of Jesus of Nazareth? Surely it is possible that someone named Jesus of Nazareth, composed of a human body and soul, could have existed without the Incarnation. Consider the following scenario. The Holy Spirit performs the act of parthenogenesis in Mary's womb. A body–soul composite is generated – the natural endowment of human nature – but is not assumed by the Word.[15] Then, this natural endowment becomes a human person, although not the God-Man. All that has to be granted here is the

---

[13] I have ignored concrete-nature views that are two-partist, because, as I pointed out in the previous chapter, these are Apollinarian.

[14] This is not to deny the pre-existence of Christ if this means the pre-existent Word. It is the Word that pre-exists the Incarnation – that is, Christ's divine nature. Perhaps the property of human nature pre-exists the Incarnation, if one is a realist about properties. But this does not necessarily mean that the Word has this property prior to the Incarnation. In fact, claiming that the Word does have all that is necessary for being human prior to the Incarnation, bar a human body, is exactly what Apollinarius taught.

[15] If traducianism is true, I presume it is not true in the case of the human soul of Christ, because Christ is traditionally said to be without sin, and any human soul *sub lapsu* that is generated from the soul of its parents would, it seems, be generated with the property of original sin. However, for an alternative view, see W. G. T. Shedd, *Dogmatic Theology*, 3rd edn (Phillipsburg, P&R Publishing Co., 2003 [1889–1894].), pp. 638 n. 72 and 639.

premise that parthenogenesis is possible without Incarnation. This seems possible. At least, there seems no obvious reason to think this could not take place.[16] We could argue that there is a possible world in which a human being is generated in the womb of Mary *Theotokos* through parthenogenesis via the Holy Spirit, without being assumed by the Word. But then it looks as though a three-part Christology does not meet the *enhypostatos* requirement of the *an–enhypostasia* distinction, because human nature is not made personal through the hypostatic union with the Word in the Incarnation.

We can reply to this objection in the following way. Assume that the Incarnation does not take place, but the divine special creation of a human nature via parthenogenesis in the womb of Mary does. ('Divine special creation' here indicates that the Holy Spirit specially intervenes in the natural order and miraculously generates a fertilized human egg in the womb of Mary, using only her human tissue to do so.) Of course, this state of affairs obtains in some possible world. It is possible that the Holy Spirit creates such a concrete particular. But it does not follow from this that what is created is the person of Christ. All that follows from this is that the Holy Spirit creates a particular human being through parthenogenesis in the womb of Mary. To see this, consider the following argument:

1. Possibly, the Holy Spirit specially creates a human body–soul composite (i.e. human nature), via parthenogenesis in the womb of Mary, that is not assumed by the Word.

[16] This should be distinguished from the idea that, without the action of the Holy Spirit in the virginal conception, Christ's human nature would not exist in order to be assumed by the Word. It is possible that the Incarnation could take place without a virgin birth. But it is not possible that the human nature of Christ, however it is generated, forms 'part' of the person of Christ without being assumed by the Word. Brian Leftow makes a similar point in 'A timeless God Incarnate', in Stephen Davis, Daniel Kendall and Gerald O'Collins (eds.), *The Incarnation* (Oxford: Oxford University Press, 2002), p. 280. It is also a staple of Protestant orthodoxy. See Heinrich Heppe, *Reformed Dogmatics*, trans. G. T. Thompson (London: Wakeman Trust, 1950), p. 416, section 7.

2. This human nature constitutes 'part' of Christ only if it is hypostatically united with the person of the Word.

3. So, the human person generated by this process is not 'part' of the God-Man.

If the Incarnation takes place, the human nature of Christ does not at any time compose an existing individual human person apart from the Word. If the Incarnation does not take place, it does not compose the individual human person that would have been composed had the Incarnation taken place, because it is not a human nature that is assumed by the Word. Moreover, if the Incarnation does not take place, but the parthenogenic act of the Holy Spirit in the womb of Mary does, the human nature thereby generated becomes a human person. (The use of 'becomes' here should not be taken to indicate a temporal lag between creation of the human nature and its personhood. The point is simply that, in this case, the human nature that would have been assumed by the Word is not assumed by the Word. As a result what is generated is *suppositum*, as the medievals would have put it – an ontologically fundamental substance – that forms a mere human person.) But then it cannot be the case that the human being that exists without the Incarnation is the person of Christ, because without an incarnation all we have are the Word and this particular human being called Jesus of Nazareth. We do not have a God-Man. So this argument does not present a problem that the three-part Christologist is unable to overcome.

Summary

We are now in a position to summarize the foregoing. It seems that versions of both the abstract-nature view and the concrete-nature view of the human nature of Christ are compatible with the Barthian account of the *an–enhypostasia* distinction. The abstract-nature view can be taken in (at least) one of two ways, depending on whether one thinks properties are universals or particulars. If the former, then the defender of this view can affirm the anhypostatic element of the *an–enhypostasia* distinction, but it turns out to be nothing more than a trivial consequence of holding the realist explanation of abstract natures. Moreover, the defenders of this account need to qualify what it means to say that the human nature of Christ was enhypostatic. I have argued that this qualification means that there is little that is theologically substantive about this understanding of the enhypostatic aspect of the distinction. Thus, although this account of Christ's human nature makes sense of one construal of the *an–enhypostasia* distinction, it does so at the cost of making the distinction seem theologically inconsequential.

Alternatively, one could opt for a trope version of the abstract-nature view. This, unlike the realist account, depends upon the metaphysical claim that no nature exists independently of a person, the reason being that properties are particulars that exist only when the person who possesses these properties exists. The upshot of this is that the *anhypostatos physis* is meaningless, but the *enhypostatos physis* is meaningful. But this will not appeal to a theologian wanting to affirm both aspects of the *an–enhypostatos* distinction. Two-part Christologists are, as far as I can see, committed to a view of human nature that will look like one of these two accounts, even if, with nominalists that are not trope theorists, the two-partist denies the existence of properties.

The alternative, favoured by those theologians who are three-part Christologists, is that human natures are concrete particulars that do not exist prior to, or independently of, the persons that possess them. In this limited respect, the three-part Christologist's understanding of Christ's human nature is similar to the trope two-part Christologist's story. (But, importantly, this need not mean that the three-part Christologist is a trope theorist or a more conventional nominalist with respect to properties, though a three-partist could be.) In the case of the Incarnation, this means that the concrete particular that is the human nature of Christ is 'personalized' through the hypostatic union with the Word, thereby preserving the enhy-postatic aspect of the *an–enhypostasia* distinction. It is also the case that if the three-part Christologist is a realist about properties, some sense can be made of the claim that Christ's human nature is anhy-postatic. Christ has those properties common to all human beings, as well as those properties particular to Christ alone, and these prop-erties are universals. Nevertheless, it is the concrete particular that is Christ's human nature that has these properties. So, this three-part account of the human nature of Christ entails that there are proper-ties that the human nature of Christ exemplifies. It also means that the human nature of Christ is 'part' of the person of the Word, who assumes this human nature at the Incarnation. This, it seems to me, makes better sense of the *an–enhypostasia* distinction than the alter-natives we have considered. And it provides a good reason – if one thinks that being able to make sense of the *an–enhypostasia* distinc-tion is a good reason – for thinking that a three-part Christology offers the best way of expounding one traditional way of thinking about the human nature of Christ, namely (a version of) the concrete-nature view.

4 | Did Christ have a *fallen* human nature?

To condemn sin does not belong to someone with a nature like ours, under the tyranny of sin, an ordinary man.

St Cyril of Alexandria

In the previous two chapters we have considered the human nature of Christ. However, we did not deal with one important issue in recent theological understandings of this doctrine, which has to do with whether or not Christ had a fallen human nature. In this chapter, we turn to this issue.

The humanity of Christ

A number of theologians of the past 200 years have maintained that Christ had a human nature that possessed the property of being fallen, but not the property of being sinful.[1] The most influential

---

[1] Karl Barth advocated this view in *Church Dogmatics*, G. W. Bromiley and T. F. Torrance, 4 vols. (Edinburgh: T. & T. Clark, 1957–1969), I/2, pp. 147–159. In the nineteenth century, Edward Irving made similar claims in *The Orthodox and Catholic Doctrine of Our Lord's Human Nature* (London: Baldwin and Cradock, 1830). Irving's discussion has been revitalized by contemporary theologians like Colin Gunton in his 'Two dogmas Revisited: Edward Irving's Christology', *Scottish Journal of Theology* 41 (1988), pp. 359–376, and Thomas Weinandy in his monograph, *In the Likeness of Sinful Flesh: an Essay on the Humanity of Christ* (Edinburgh: T. & T. Clark, 1993). There are a number of Eastern Orthodox theologians who have taken this position on Christ's humanity. However, I shall restrict this chapter to discussion of Western theologians, particularly (though, not exclusively) in the Reformed tradition.

among them is Karl Barth. He says: 'There must be no weakening or obscuring of the saving truth that the nature which God assumed in Christ is identical with our nature as we see it in the light of the Fall. If it were otherwise, how could Christ be really like us? What concern would we have with him? We stand before God characterised by the Fall. God's Son not only assumed our nature but he entered the concrete form of our nature, under which we stand before God as men damned and lost.'[2]

This view has also found support among a number of more recent theologians. One such is J. B. Torrance: 'As Edward Irving the great Scottish theologian in the early nineteenth century and Karl Barth in our own day have said . . . Christ assumed 'fallen humanity' that our humanity might be turned back to God in him by his sinless life in the Spirit, and, through him, in us.'[3]

This, it is claimed, safeguards the true humanity of Christ and his identification with fallen human beings in the Incarnation, while upholding the sinless integrity of his divinity. For these reasons (among others), defenders of this view claim that it is to be preferred to the idea that Christ was either sinless (without sin) or impeccable (incapable of sinning), and possessed a human nature that was unfallen. (The notion that Christ was sinless or impeccable is said to jeopardize the true humanity of Christ, who – so the argument goes – is neither truly identified with fallen humanity in their fallenness, nor, in the case of the impeccability, truly subject to temptation as other humans are.) In what follows, we shall refer to the claim that Christ's human nature had the property of being fallen as the 'fallenness' view, and the notion that Christ's human nature had the property of being unfallen as the 'sinlessness' view. (I suppose one could claim Christ's *human* nature was impeccable, as opposed to saying that his theanthropic *person* is impeccable because of the

[2] Barth, *Church Dogmatics*, 1/2, p. 153.

[3] J. B. Torrance, 'The vicarious humanity of Christ', in T. F. Torrance (ed.), *The Incarnation* (Edinburgh: Handsel Press, 1981), p. 141.

presence of the Word, sanctifying or preserving inviolate the human nature of Christ. But then it would be very difficult to make sense of the biblical idea that he was truly tempted. In order to make matters easier, I shall not speak of Christ's human nature in this fashion).[4]

Unfortunately, defenders of this fallenness view of Christ's human nature are not always very clear in their articulation of the fallenness position.[5] Yet, despite this, the fallenness view has been espoused by an impressive range of contemporary theologians, particularly among those in the Reformed tradition. For this reason, it is worth considering the coherence of this controversial claim, in order to ascertain whether some sense can be made of it.

We shall set about achieving this objective in three stages. In the first, we shall look at the theological problem original sin poses for defenders of the fallenness view. In the second stage, we shall use the concepts outlined in discussing the traditional doctrine of original sin in order to set forth one version of the fallenness view that seems, *prima facie*, to overcome these problems. Although this doctrine would not be endorsed by most of those who defend the fallenness view, it has the merit of making sense of a fallen human nature that is without actual sin. In the third stage, the discussion of original sin in the first stage will be applied to the argument in defence of the fallenness view outlined in the second stage. We shall see that

[4] And another thing: it might be thought meaningless to ask the question, 'Did Christ have a fallen human nature?', if human nature is just a property. A set of properties cannot be fallen, but persons can be. I suppose someone sympathetic to the view that Christ's human nature is a property could say that one of the properties, or property-conjuncts, included in Christ's human nature was the property 'being fallen'. In any case, I have defended the view that Christ's human nature is a concrete particular. One can say of a certain sort of concrete particular that it has the moral property 'being fallen'.

[5] Compare Kelly Kapic's comment. 'We must conclude by demonstrating that the issues at hand are less clear than sometimes acknowledged, requiring more than simply an affirmation of whether the Son assumes a *fallen* or *unfallen* nature. Given the lack of clear and agreed definitions, claiming one position or the other does not actually convey much of theological substance.' 'The Son's assumption of a human nature: a call for clarity', *International Journal for Systematic Theology* 14 (2001), pp. 163–164.

this defence does not succeed, for reasons laid out in the initial discussion of original sin. In fact, there does not seem to be any way of making sense of the notion that Christ had a human nature that had the property of being fallen but not the property of being sinful, the reason being that 'fallenness' is traditionally understood as the condition of being sinful.[6] And no substantive meaning can be given to the notion of 'fallenness' that does not entail this sinfulness, even in some weak, non-culpable form. All of which appears to have grave consequences for the fallenness view.

Fallenness and original sin

All orthodox theologians maintain that Christ's human nature had the property of being sinless, including defenders of the fallenness view (for whom Christ's human nature is *fallen* but not *sinful*).[7] It is not hard to understand why: Hebrews 4.15 states: 'We do not have a High Priest who cannot sympathize with our weaknesses, but one who was was in all points tempted as we are, *yet without sin*.' Up until the nineteenth century, many if not most theologians in the Western tradition understood this to entail that Christ's human nature did not possess the property of fallenness.[8] The reasons for this devolve upon the doctrine of original sin. Traditional formulations of the doctrine of original sin rule out the possibility that Christ could have a human nature with the property of fallenness. The reasons for this

---

[6] A similar point is made by Donald Macleod in discussing Edward Irving's version of the fallenness view. He says Irving's doctrine 'requires that original sin should be ascribed to Christ; for original sin is a vice of fallen human nature; and the doctrine that our Lord's human nature was fallen means, if it means anything, that it was tainted with original sin.' *The Person of Christ* (Leicester: Inter-Varsity Press, 1998), pp. 228–229.

[7] Richard Sturch observes that one of the problems besetting discussions of this nature is the fact that there has been no agreed definition of what original sin consists in, in the Christian tradition. See his *The Word and The Christ: An Essay in Analytic Christology* (Oxford: Oxford University Press, 1991), Excursus 4, p. 262. This is true, although all orthodox theologians would agree that, whatever original sin is, Christ must be sinless.

[8] Weinandy disputes this in *In the Likeness of Sinful Flesh*.

can be set forth fairly easily. Let us take these two issues in reverse, beginning with the human nature of Christ, before turning to an exposition of the position of one version of the doctrine of original sin that can be found in Reformed orthodoxy.

In keeping with previous chapters, I shall assume that Christ's human nature is a concrete particular, composed of a body and soul distinct from the Word. This appears to be what the Reformed orthodox believed, (although not all post-Reformation Reformed theologians state unequivocally which view in particular they hold to).[9] It is also commensurate with the claim that the human nature of Christ has certain essential properties, and certain contingent ones. Jesus of Nazareth, like all human beings, may gain or lose contingent properties (such as having a right arm, or possessing a good memory), but may not gain or lose one or more of his essential properties and remain the same concrete individual. Such essential properties a particular human being possesses might include having a particular soul, having a particular parentage, or having a particular genetic code. In addition to having a particular human nature, let us presume that each human person (Christ included) belongs to the natural kind 'humanity'. This means that, in addition to the properties that this particular individual human being has, such as

---

[9] See, for example, Heinrich Heppe, *Reformed Dogmatics*, trans. G. T. Thompson (London: Wakeman Trust, 1950), p. 416: 'The humanity taken up into the personality of the Logos is . . . thought of in its full spirit–body essentiality and individuality.' Bartholomaeus Keckermann in particular seems to lift a medieval understanding of Christ's human nature almost verbatim into his own writing on the subject (p. 417, citing Keckermann, *Systema Sacrosanctae Theologiae: Tribus Libris Adornatum* (Geneva, 1611), p. 315). Similarly, Francis Turretin speaks of the Word assuming 'not human nature in general, but in particular a nature derived from Adam'. See *Institutes of Elenctic Theology*, II, trans. George Musgrave Giger, ed. James T. Dennison Jr (Phillipsburg: P&R Publishing Co., 1992), 13.5.7, p. 308. Professor Richard Muller has informed me (in private correspondence) that all the Reformed orthodox and probably all (or almost all) the Lutheran orthodox took a hylomorphic view of the body–soul relation, often in conscious opposition to the Cartesian version of substance dualism. In which case, all the Reformed orthodox thought of Christ's human nature as a concrete particular.

'being born to Mary in a stable in Bethlehem in 4 BC' every human will have a certain number of properties in common with all other human beings, such as 'being composed of a body and soul' or 'being made in the image of God'. (Of course, this presupposes that some version of realism rather than some version of nominalism is true.) Now, the property 'being fallen' or 'fallenness' is not an essential property of all human beings *per se*. That is, it is not a property that an entity has to exemplify in order to be counted part of a particular kind (of thing), in this case the kind 'humanity'. It is not essential to being human that a particular human is fallen. This would appear to be theologically uncontroversial, since at least one human being, Adam, existed *before* the Fall. Prior to the Fall Adam could not have had the property 'being fallen' any more than I can have the property 'being forty years old' prior to my fortieth birthday. Therefore, 'being fallen' is not essential to the kind 'humanity'. It cannot be part of what it means to be human.

It has been argued by a number of classical theologians that Christ had a human nature similar to Adam's human nature prior to the Fall.[10] This would mean that Christ's human nature was able not to sin (*posse non peccare*) and, as a consequence of remaining in this state, was sin*less*. Theologians in the Augustinian tradition maintain

---

[10] In this chapter I shall use a number of terms to refer to distinct but interrelated theological positions. 'Classical' theology is used here interchangeably with 'Augustinian' theology since, arguably, Augustinian theology (of various hues) is the majority report in the Christian tradition. I shall also refer to 'Reformed' theology, 'Reformed scholasticism' and 'Reformed orthodoxy'. These all refer to the same theological tradition. This is the tradition of Calvinistic theology that grew up post-Reformation and adopted the elenctic methods of the medieval schoolmen. In the recent literature on this movement a distinction is made between Reformed (and Protestant) scholasticism as a theological method, and Reformed (and Protestant) orthodoxy, the content of the dogmatic systems espoused by these theologians. For more on these distinctions, see the Introduction to William J. van Asselt and Eef Dekker (eds.), *Reformation and Scholasticism: An Ecumenical Enterprise* (Grand Rapids: Baker Academic, 2001). One proponent of the view that Christ had a human nature like Adam is William Shedd. See his *Dogmatic Theology*, 3rd edn (Phillipsburg: P&R Publishing Co., 2003 [1889–1894]), part 5.

the stronger thesis that, although Christ's human nature was able to sin in and of itself, it was incapable of sinning (*non posse peccare*) because of its union with the Word, and as a result of this, impeccable. Briefly, what this means is that, although Christ's human nature was constituted such that it was capable of sinning, it was rendered incapable of sinning by virtue of its hypostatic union with the Word. So the human nature with which the impeccable Word is in hypostatic union in the Incarnation will be prevented from sinning by the Word, even though, in abstraction from the Word (so to speak), the human nature of Christ is able to sin. Nevertheless, for the purposes of this argument we shall suppose that Christ has a 'fallen' human nature, as classical theologians maintained all human beings have post-Fall (usually with the exception of Christ). This means granting, for the present, the supposition that Christ could have a human nature that was fallen but not sinful, and allowing that this is a meaningful distinction to make.

Next, we need to explain something of the classical doctrine of original sin. The medieval schoolmen distinguished two aspects to original sin: hereditary corruption (*corruptio hereditaria*) and hereditary guilt (*culpa hereditaria*). However, most of those in the Reformed tradition have rejected the notion of *inherited* corruption and guilt in favour of *imputed* corruption and guilt.[11] The majority opinion among the Reformed was that these two aspects of original sin were directly, or immediately, imputed to all of Adam's posterity after the Fall. They were not imparted mediately, through natural generation (although this was the opinion of the Saumur School of Reformed theology, following Placaeus[12]). We shall refer to original corruption and original guilt, rather than to inherited corruption and inherited

---

[11] Shedd is an exception to this. In his *Dogmatic Theology* he defends Augustinian realism and inherited sin. Another exception is his contemporary, the Baptist theologian Augustus Strong.

[12] For more on the difference between mediate and immediate imputation see Oliver D. Crisp, 'On the theological pedigree of Jonathan Edwards's doctrine of imputation', *Scottish Journal of Theology* 56 (2003), pp. 308–327.

guilt, in keeping with (most of) the Reformed orthodox, rather than medieval, tradition. (The related problems associated with the mechanism of imputing sin and guilt will be passed over in silence.)

Original corruption involves a propensity or proneness to actual sin, but is not the same as actual sin.[13] In the same way, a person might have a proneness to drink too much wine when it is offered to him. But this is not the same as that person actually giving in to this propensity and drinking too much wine when it is offered to him. This proneness to sin inclines human beings to sin, but it does not necessitate that they do sin on any particular occasion. (Of course, the same could be said for the wine-bibber.) Nevertheless, it is usually thought that human beings who possess original corruption will, at some point in their lives, commit an actual sin as a result of this proneness to sin. Similarly, those with a propensity to intoxication will probably, other things being equal, act upon that proneness at some point in their lives (though, of course, they need not, and may not). That is, persons with such proneness will (probably) sin on at least one occasion. Augustinian theologians (including those in the classical Reformed tradition) go further and state that human beings will *inevitably* sin, where they possess original corruption, without the intervention of divine grace.[14] Let us assume that divine grace does not normally intervene to prevent actual sin from taking place in the case of human beings with original corruption. Then, such human beings inevitably sin (at least once).[15]

---

[13] The Westminster Shorter Catechism states in answer to Question 18: 'The sinfulness of that first estate whereinto man fell consists of the guilt of Adam's first sin, the want of original righteousness, and the corruption of the whole nature: which is commonly called original sin; together with all actual transgressions which proceed from it.' I am not including actual transgression as a distinct aspect of the notion of original sin. Strictly speaking, actual sin is a consequence of original sin; it is not part of original sin.

[14] This point is made by Richard Swinburne in *Responsibility and Atonement* (Oxford: Oxford University Press, 1989), p. 138.

[15] Of course, the Reformed orthodox would not agree to the qualifier 'at least once'. There might be an even stronger position than this. It could be argued that every

Original guilt, the other component of a traditional doctrine of original sin, has proved more controversial, particularly in the recent literature. Richard Swinburne is one contemporary philosophical theologian who rejects it in his account of original sin, retaining only inherited (as opposed to original) corruption as a sort of genetic vitiation that is propagated, but not, as with Pelagianism, imitated.[16] In other words, inherited corruption is passed down the generations through biological propagation,[17] not through the perpetuation of sinful social practices, imitated by one generation from the previous generation.[18]

There are good reasons to be suspicious about the coherence of inherited guilt. The principal problem with it is that guilt does not seem to be a notion that admits of transfer from one person to

action of a sinful human being is tainted by sin such that no act of a sinful human being can ever be pleasing to God, and every act by such human beings is offensive to God. How would every act be offensive to God? Perhaps if every act of a sinful human is not properly orientated towards glorifying God in some way it would be offensive to God. Or maybe it is because every act is tainted by sin that it is offensive to God. We shall return to this issue later in the discussion.

[16] Pelagianism is the notion that human beings have libertarian free will, and are not subject to original sin.

[17] This sounds like the Tridentine position on original sin. The third canon of the Council of Trent on original sin states: 'If anyone asserts that this sin of Adam, which is one by origin, and which is communicated to all men by propagation, not by imitation (*propagatione, non imitatione transfusum*), and which is in all men and proper to each [is removed either by some power of human nature or by any other means than the merit of our Lord Jesus Christ] . . . let him be anathema.' Henricus Denzinger and Adolfus Schönmetzer (eds.), *Enchiridion Symbolorum: Definitionum et Declarationium de Rebus: Fidei et Morum.* 32nd edn (Freiburg: Herder, 1963), p. 1513, cited by George Vandervelde in *Original Sin: Two Major Trends in Contemporary Roman Catholic Reinterpretation* (Lanham: University Press of America, 1981), p. 36.

[18] Barth also had reservations about original guilt. He sought to rethink the doctrine of original sin without recourse to the traditional theological apparatus of imputed or inherited sin. See John Webster, *Barth's Moral Theology: Human Action in Barth's Moral Thought* (Edinburgh: T. & T. Clark, 1998), ch. 4, and Barth, *Church Dogmatics* IV/ 2, pp. 500 ff.

another. Whereas punishment may be transferred, guilt may not. A simple example will make the point. Trevor steals a watch from a jeweller and is caught red-handed by a policeman. The penalty for his crime is a fine of £100, which Trevor is unable to pay, because he is penniless. Happily for him, however, his friend Gary is willing and able to pay the fine, and, as a result of his intervention, Trevor is set at liberty once more. However, although Gary has paid Trevor's fine, he has not thereby erased Trevor's guilt. Nor has Trevor's guilt passed to Gary by virtue of Gary's paying the fine owed by Trevor. Trevor remains the guilty party, since it was Trevor who committed the crime. This remains true whatever Gary may do on Trevor's behalf, however extravagant or generous he may be. Although Gary can, in certain circumstances, take on Trevor's punishment, he may not take on Trevor's guilt. This sort of thought-experiment may provide grounds for claiming that guilt is in principle non-transferable.[19] In which case, the notion of *imputed* guilt is problematic, if it is the case that the guilt pertaining to Adam's first sin cannot be transferred from Adam to anyone else. (Of course, defenders of the Reformed doctrine of imputed sin and guilt will dispute this, but at the least, this shows that there is a serious problem that the doctrine faces.)

In medieval scholastic theology, the notion of original guilt was subdivided into two aspects. The first of these is inherited guilt. This comprises two parts: (a) the *reatus culpae* (liability to guilt), which denotes that by which a person is unworthy of divine grace, and counted worthy of divine wrath and punishment, and (b) the *reatus poenae* (liability to punishment), which denotes that by which a person is subject to condemnation. In extrapolating this distinction, the medievals claimed that God may remit the *reatus culpae* through

---

[19] I have not provided a more comprehensive argument for my claims about inherited guilt since this would take us beyond the scope of this essay. The problem has been discussed by William Wainwright in 'Original sin', in Thomas V. Morris (ed.), *Philosophy and the Christian Faith* (Notre Dame: University of Notre Dame Press, 1988), pp. 31–60.

the work of Christ (*obedientia Christi*). However, they also claimed that the *reatus poenae* is not remitted by the work of Christ, but may be satisfied by, for example, a moral life or a punishment served, such as time spent in purgatory.

An example may make this distinction clearer. Let us say that a man commits murder, but repents and becomes a Christian. God forgives the man his sin through the work of Christ, such that the man's liability to guilt (*reatus culpae*) for that sin is dealt with. But he still has to serve a custodial sentence for his crime, thereby paying the penalty due his sin (*reatus poenae*). In this instance, the man has his sin forgiven him, and the liability to guilt that goes with this removed or remitted. But he still has the liability to punishment that must be served in gaol.

A similar thought experiment might be used to show that persons could have liability to guilt removed in the case of sin against God, (blasphemy, say). But such persons would still have the liability to punishment that is not remitted by Christ's work, and might, on the understanding of the medievals, lead them to be punished for their sin in purgatory. Nevertheless, in this situation the persons concerned will not be finally condemned for their sin, since the liability to guilt has been remitted through the work of Christ. But they still may have a sentence to serve prior to entry into heaven. (A biblical example of this might be King David and the death of his firstborn with Bathsheba, a punishment for the sin of adultery in 2 Samuel 12. It appears that God removed David's guilt but served the punishment for sin upon David. The guilt for his sin was removed; but the penal consequence of that sin was still enforced.)

The Reformed orthodox rejected this distinction, positing potential and actual guilt (*reatus potentialis* and *actualis*) in place of these two notions.[20] We can express their position in the following manner.

---

[20] Richard Muller says: 'The Protestant scholastics refused to separate *poena* and *culpa* in this manner, and therefore refuse to make a distinction between *reatus culpae* and *reatus poenae*. Instead, they argue a single *reatus*, or liability, on the basis of the fall, a

First, there are two aspects to original (that is, immediately imputed as opposed to inherited) guilt. These are: (a) the *reatus potentialis* (potential guilt), which denotes the intrinsic desert of punishment that is inseparable from sin and is non-transferable, and (b) the *reatus actualis* (actual guilt), which denotes that aspect of guilt that is transferable and can be remitted by divine mercy.

The problem with the medieval view, according to the Reformed orthodox, was that it meant that the *reatus* (liability or propensity) that accompanies the *macula* (vitiated nature) of original sin simply *is* the obligation to punish a person because of his or her culpability. In which case, removal of liability to culpability entails removal of liability to punishment. For example, Francis Turretin:

> Since culpability and punishment are related and guilt is nothing else than the obligation to punishment arising from culpability, they mutually posit and remove each other so that culpability and its guilt being removed, the punishment itself ought to be taken away necessarily (as it can be inflicted only on account of culpability). Otherwise culpability cannot be said to be remitted or its guilt taken away, if there still remains something to be purged from the sinner because of it.[21]

Turretin and the other Reformed orthodox maintained that the medieval distinction between *reatus culpae* and *poenae* is simply mistaken in bifurcating guilt in the manner in which it does. If guilt requires punishment, then no meaning can be given to a notion that seeks to distinguish them. Hence, in place of the medieval distinction, the Reformed orthodox spoke of potential and actual guilt as the two component parts of original guilt.

---

liability to both guilt and punishment.' Muller, *Dictionary of Latin and Greek Theological Terms* (Grand Rapids: Baker, 1985), p. 258, S. V. 'Reatus; reatus poenae'. This point is echoed by Heppe in *Reformed Dogmatics*, p. 326: 'A distinction is drawn between *reatus potentialis* and *actualis* [potential and actual sin]; on the other hand the scholastic distinction between *reatus culpae* and *poenae* is rejected.'

[21] Turretin, *Institutes of Elenctic Theology*, II, 9.4, pp. 595–596.

In the mid-twentieth century, the Reformed theologian Louis Berkhof took a slightly different position from the Reformed orthodox, which appears more in keeping with the language of the medieval schoolmen, although utilized for his own (Reformed) purposes. He argues that liability to guilt (*reatus culpae*) is non-transferable and is of the essence of sin even though God may forgive sinners their sin. But liability to punishment (*reatus poenae*) is transferable, relates to the penal sanction of the law and is therefore not of the essence of sin. Thus Berkhof:

> By this [liability to punishment] is meant desert of punishment, or obligation to render satisfaction to God's justice for self-determined violation of the law. Guilt in this sense is not of the essence of sin, but is rather a relation to the penal sanction of the law. If there had been no sanction attached to the disregard of moral relations, every departure from the law would have been sin, but would not have involved liability to punishment. Guilt in this sense may be removed by the satisfaction of justice, either personally or vicariously. It may be transferred from one person to another, or assumed by one person for another.[22]

This means that a person could be guilty of a sin even where that sin is not punishable. A person could be guilty of bigamy, say, in a society where bigamy is not punishable by law. Similarly, a person could be guilty of sinning against God, and that guilt remain (because it is non-transferable), though God forgives this person through the work of Christ. Such a person would be forgiven the guilt of his or her sin (*reatus culpae*) though the *reatus* remains even after forgiveness. But the punishment he or she would have suffered had the sin not been forgiven (*reatus poenae*) is remitted because of the work of Christ.

The nineteenth-century Princetonian theologian Charles Hodge defends precisely this view in the following terms:

---

[22] Louis Berkhof, *Systematic Theology* (Edinburgh: Banner of Truth, 1939), p. 246.

A man condemned at a human tribunal for any offence against the community, when he has endured the penalty which the law prescribes, is no less unworthy, his demerit as much exists as it did from the beginning; but his liability to justice or obligation to the penalty of the law, in other words, his guilt in that sense of the word, is removed. It would be unjust to punish him a second time for that offence.[23]

We might express this distinction according to the doctrine of the immediate imputation of original sin as follows. All human beings post-Fall have imputed to them Adam's guilt, and, as a consequence of this, Adam's corruption. It is not the case that all post-Fall humanity has a corrupt nature passed down to it via natural generation, and, as a consequence of this, incurs an inherited guilt. This is the mediate-imputation doctrine, and it would mean that original corruption logically precedes and is the ground of original guilt.[24] Instead, guilt is logically prior to corruption, according to immediate imputation. But, as Berkhof and Hodge show, original guilt has two aspects that need to be distinguished: liability to guilt, and liability to punishment. This liability to punishment is a logical consequence of the liability to guilt. It could be said that liability to punishment supervenes upon liability to guilt, and that original corruption, at least,

---

[23] Charles Hodge, *Systematic Theology*, II (Edinburgh: Thomas Nelson, 1874), 8.7, p. 189. It seems that Berkhof has taken his own views from Hodge's discussion of the same issue, although Berkhof does not credit Hodge as the source of his own position. I am indebted to Dr Daniel Hill for pointing this out to me.

[24] Could there be a hybrid of these two views? Could it be that original corruption logically precedes original guilt, where both aspects of original sin are immediately imputed to Adam's posterity? Perhaps. The Reformed orthodox rejected any notion that guilt was logically contingent upon corruption, because it is *Adam's* sin that is immediately imputed, and, in Adam's case, guilt (for sin) logically precedes the corruption of his nature. He is corrupt because he is guilty of sin; he is not guilty of sin because he is corrupt. If it is Adam's sinful nature that is immediately imputed to his posterity, then the same logical priority applies to original sin: Adam's posterity has original guilt and corruption imputed immediately to it, but the guilt logically precedes and grounds the corrupt nature.

on the doctrine of immediate imputation, supervenes upon original guilt. Thus, although the Reformed orthodox rejected the medieval distinction between *reatus culpae* and *reatus poenae*, this distinction does serve a useful purpose in differentiating between the logical components of original guilt and original corruption.

So, to sum up, the classical Reformed doctrine of original sin comprises both original corruption and original guilt. However, there seem to be considerable problems with the notion of inherited guilt, problems that would also pertain to original guilt, viz. the transference problem. It may be that, if no solution to this problem in the traditional doctrine of original sin is forthcoming, original guilt needs to be excised from original sin. This would have important implications for the logic of immediate imputation. If there is no such thing as original guilt, then it would seem that the corrupt nature that post-Fall human beings possess is not, strictly speaking, a nature for which any post-Fall human being is culpable. This would be extremely problematic for the classical Reformed doctrine with respect to the imputation of original sin to fallen humanity. But it may be conducive to our concerns with Christ's fallen humanity, since, if a plausible version of original sin without original guilt can be defended in the case of Christ's human nature, then there may be grounds for an argument in favour of the notion of Christ having a fallen human nature. We shall not consider whether the traditional Reformed doctrine of original sin, in its application to fallen humanity *per se*, is coherent or not. Instead, we shall focus on whether the doctrine of original sin can be revised in order to make sense of the claim that Christ's humanity might be fallen. This involves removing the element of original guilt.[25]

---

[25] It seems to me that, as it stands, the traditional Reformed doctrine of original sin is deeply flawed. (This does not mean that the doctrine of original sin is deeply flawed; only that this version of the doctrine is.) However, there may be ways of reviving the Reformed view, or articulating a doctrine very similar in many respects. For instance,

Before turning to consider an argument in defence of the fallenness view of Christ's humanity along these lines, we need to examine one further question with regard to the Reformed orthodox doctrine of original sin. It is this: does possession of original corruption, even in the absence of original guilt, mean that the person in possession of such a condition is liable to be damned? The answer appears to be in the affirmative. To make this clear, consider the following scenario. Let us assume, as defenders of the traditional view of original sin we are considering would have done, that God's punishment of sin is essentially retributive, in which case the punishment God serves upon sin must fit the crime committed.[26] Now, in a particular world, w1, God brings about the creation of beings to which the sin of the first human creature is imputed. However, this imputation involves only the first component of the traditional doctrine of original sin, that is, original corruption. So, in w1, as a result of Adam's sin, God imputes original corruption, but not original guilt, to all of Adam's posterity. Now, Trevor is one of Adam's (fallen) posterity in w1. Does this mean that Trevor in w1 is worthy of punishment merely on the basis of possessing original corruption? Perhaps not: if he has no original guilt, then he cannot have *reatus culpae* or *reatus poenae*. And if he has neither aspect of original guilt, then it does not seem that he is culpable for possessing original corruption. However, he could still be loathsome to God in virtue of being corrupt. This would be the case even if he never actually sins. It is no defence, in this situation, to claim that if a person never actually sins because, say, he is prevented from doing so by dying at birth, he is free from actual sin (and, being a citizen of w1, from original guilt) and therefore not

it may be that God does not need to 'impute' original sin to fallen humanity, because all human beings are one metaphysical entity, in which case Adam and his posterity really do share in the same sinfulness. Augustine advocates a view similar to this one in *City of God* 12.3.

[26] I have considered divine retributive punishment at greater length in 'Divine retribution: a defence', *Sophia* 42 (2003), pp. 35–52.

punishable by God in hell. For God could refuse such an individual a place in heaven even should the individual never actually sin, or have original guilt, merely because, in virtue of having a fallen human nature (original corruption), he is loathsome to God and must have the blessings of heaven withheld from him.

So, it seems that if a human person had original corruption but not original guilt (assuming that these two concepts are not entailed – something some Reformed theologians might disagree with), and was to be prevented (by some circumstance, or other agent) from committing actual sin (whether intentionally or unintentionally), that person would still be loathsome to God, and, as a consequence of that, excluded from heaven. We might say that, even if fallenness entails only that a human person has original corruption and not original guilt, such persons are still excluded from heaven, even if they are not, strictly speaking, *guilty* of possessing original corruption. But what we must say, according to Reformed orthodoxy, is that being fallen entails being sinful (that is, having the property of original sin). Even if a person only has original corruption and never actually sins, possession of original corruption is itself sinful, and therefore loathsome in the sight of God, because possession of an originally corrupt human nature entails possession of a morally corrupt human nature. And, to be fallen, a human being must have at least this component of original sin, whether or not such a being also has the two component parts of original guilt.

In defence of the fallenness view

With this discussion of the traditional doctrine of original sin in view, we may proceed to set forth an argument for the conclusion that Christ's human nature had the property of fallenness. The defenders of the fallenness view of whom I am aware would all want to affirm Chalcedonian Christology, whether or not they are also committed to a concrete-nature view of Christ's human nature. But let us assume that defenders of the fallenness view want to hold to this view of the human nature of Christ as one aspect of their understanding of Chalcedonian Christology. Now, quite clearly, the most contentious aspect of the fallenness view lies at the very heart of what it seeks to show: that it can make sense both of a Chalcedonian Christology *and* of Christ possessing a fallen, but not sinful, human nature. The fallenness doctrine depends upon Christ sharing the property 'being fallen' with *all* other human beings after the fall of Adam. If Christ is to redeem human beings from their fallen condition, so, defenders of this view often say, he must share this condition in order to redeem it, much as, one might think, a scientist might infect himself with a disease in order to test a vaccine. But this seems impossible, for reasons that will shortly become clear. Nevertheless, for the sake of the argument, let us grant to Irving, Barth, J. B. Torrance and those sympathetic to this view, the assumption that, in principle, it is possible for Christ to be fallen without being sinful, and that this could be expressed in a way compatible with Chalcedonian Christology.

The next stage of the argument is to see that if Christ has the property of being fallen, then he has the property of original sin. As we saw in the first section of the chapter, the notion that fallenness requires original sin seems to be the overwhelming affirmation of classical theology in the West until the nineteenth century and the development of the fallenness view in Christology.[27] That is, those theologians who speak of human beings after the fall as having a human nature with the property of fallenness mean by this that any such human being has the property of original sin. Indeed, it seems that part of the very notion of fallenness is that a person who is fallen is sinful in some way. From our discussion of the classical views of original sin it is clear that if Christ has original sin, then he has both original corruption and original guilt. The problem with this is that

---

[27] We have already noted that Thomas Weinandy disputes this. His book *In the Likeness of Sinful Flesh* is an apology for the fallenness view, in which he claims that it has a long history in Scripture and the Western theological tradition. But this is contentious.

if Christ has original sin, then he shares original guilt with the rest of humanity post-Fall, and is thereby culpable.

Thus far, what we have is entirely in accord with the traditional, Reformed articulation of original sin. If Christ shares in original sin because he has a fallen human nature, then, on this argument, he is sinful. Once his 'fallen' humanity has been granted, it is a short step to extrapolate what that involves, namely, the full-strength doctrine of original sin, and from there, to the conclusion that Christ must therefore be sinful. This obtains, on classical theology, even if Christ were never actually to sin. That is, even if Christ were simply to have a human nature that had the property of fallenness, and never once acted upon the propensity original corruption generates towards actual sin, he would still be culpable, the reason being that, as we have already noted in expounding the traditional doctrine of original sin, possession of original corruption is itself culpable in virtue of original guilt. So, a classical understanding of original sin, coupled with a commitment to the fallenness view of Christ's humanity, yields the conclusion that Christ's human nature has the property of sinfulness.

Clearly, this is not acceptable to any theologian wishing to remain credally orthodox. But is this the only way that a fallenness view can be construed? No, it is not. Consider the following variation on the argument just outlined. The contentious move was made at the point when it was affirmed that if Christ's human nature has the property of being fallen, then it has original sin. None of the defenders of a fallenness view of Christ's humanity whom I have read would affirm this, for the very reason that it commits them to the claim that Christ is sinful, which is clearly unorthodox. However, it is not clear in the writings of such theologians quite how they expect to avoid this problem. One solution would be to retain the doctrine of original corruption, as Swinburne does, while rejecting the notion of original guilt on the grounds that it is incoherent, or uncongenial to a fallenness view. Were the defenders of the fallenness doctrine to take this view, they could make a case for Christ's human nature having both the property of fallenness and (as a result) the property of original sin, without maintaining that Christ has the property of being guilty of actually sinning.

Let us elaborate such an argument. It might be that possession of a fallen human nature, meaning a human nature that has original sin, does not necessarily entail that Christ is *guilty* of being sinful. This is true if Christ may possess the property of original sin without original guilt. But how could this be? Perhaps because original guilt is incoherent, which I have already suggested is the case according to at least one form of the doctrine of original sin. In which case, all that original sin consists in is original corruption. Christ could have original corruption, it might be thought, because this implies no guilt on his part: it is non-culpable, the 'culpability aspect' (original guilt) having been excised from the doctrine. Or it may be that original guilt is merely extremely implausible, just as time-travel to the future may not be incoherent or impossible, but is extremely implausible. Then, we might think we have no strong reasons for believing that original sin has to be accompanied by original guilt. In which case, perhaps Christ could have one aspect of the doctrine and not the other. Or, it might be that original guilt makes perfect sense, but that it is simply not imputed to, or inherited by, Christ. Whether or not original guilt makes sense, all that the argument requires is that original corruption be imputed without original guilt. It seems, *prima facie*, plausible to think that original corruption might obtain without an accompanying original guilt.

At this point, the defender of a fallenness doctrine will have to choose between the weaker and the stronger version of original corruption, mentioned earlier. To recap, these were,

> *Weak original corruption* – human beings post-Fall actually sin because of original corruption, without the prevenient grace of God.
>
> *Strong original corruption* – human beings post-Fall *inevitably* actually sin because of original corruption, without the prevenient grace of God.

There is a stronger version of original corruption than this. One might claim that all actions of fallen human beings are sinful without the intervention of divine grace because they are not directed towards the glory of God in every respect. For instance, Jonathan Edwards says:

> Let it be supposed, that some beings, by natural instinct, or by some other means, have a determination of mind to union and benevolence to a particular person, or private system, which is but a small part of the universal system of being . . . this disposition or determination of mind is independent on [sic], or not subordinate to, benevolence to being in general. Such a determination, disposition, or affection of mind is not of the nature of true virtue . . . [unless it is] subordinate to benevolence to being in general.[28]

This need not mean that *all* actions of human beings post-Fall are sinful, only those not directed towards 'benevolence to being in general', identified by Edwards with God. But it might be claimed (though Edwards does not say this here) that all actions of human beings with original corruption are sinful because they are bound over to benevolence to private systems or particular persons, not to being in general, or at least not primarily, perhaps even pre-eminently, to being in general. However, since this is a more controversial view than the strong inherited-corruption claim, and since it would require further argument to defend the proposition that all the actions of fallen humans are sinful, I shall not pursue this option further here. All that is needed in this argument are the weak and the strong versions of the original-corruption claim.

By contrast to the strong and very strong versions of original corruption, the weak version of original corruption makes no claim about the inevitability of actual sin, only that it is a consequence (but not a necessary consequence) of possessing original corruption.

---

[28] Jonathan Edwards, *The Nature of True Virtue*, in *The Works of Jonathan Edwards*, I, ed. Edward Hickman (Edinburgh: Banner of Truth, 1988 [1834]), p. 126.

Defenders of a 'fallenness' view of Christ's human nature may, therefore, endorse a weak view of original corruption, taking as a concomitant of this the idea that Christ's human nature has, because of its possession of original corruption, the propensity or disposition to commit actual sin. In this moral state, and in abstraction from the divine nature, the human nature of Christ has the propensity actually to sin, although it may not do so, on any particular occasion. And, as the human nature of God Incarnate, it is not possible that this propensity to sin is ever acted upon. For any possible actual sin that the human nature of Christ would succumb to, the divine nature prevents this outcome.

So, on this argument, even if the human nature of Christ possesses weak original corruption (and it is possible for the Word to unite himself to an originally corrupt human nature), it is not possible for this human nature to sin, though *qua* human nature it has such a propensity. This involves a commitment to Christ having one aspect of original sin, that is, (weak) inherited corruption. But, since sinfulness seems to be part of the notion of fallenness, or is entailed by it, it appears that defenders of fallenness simply have to bite the bullet on this aspect of the problem. Christ may have had a fallen humanity that had original corruption but not original guilt. What is more, because of his divine nature Christ never actually sinned.

Problems with the argument

However, this argument for the fallenness of Christ's humanity has a number of very serious defects that make it unworkable for a Chalcedonian Christologist.

First, on this argument, Christ would be sinful. This, it need hardly be said, is a serious problem, since if Christ has a human nature with the (dispositional) property of sinfulness, then it is not clear how he is able to act as a redeemer, along the lines envisaged in classical theology despite the fact that there is no agreed understanding of the atonement in the tradition. Theologians are divided on the theory of atonement, but (at least among classical theologians) agreed on the Chalcedonian definition, that Christ is like other human beings in every way, sin excepted. So, a sinful Christ is simply unorthodox. This alone is fatal to the argument.

Secondly, even if Christ has only original corruption and not original guilt, this means that his human nature has the property of being morally vitiated, and, given the argument mounted in the first stage of this chapter, is thereby loathsome in the sight of his heavenly Father, even if, strictly speaking, he is not morally culpable for having this property. In the language of scholastic theology, Christ's humanity has a *macula*, or deformity of soul, because of original corruption. This in itself is sinful and would prevent Christ from entering heaven, since, as we noted previously, God may withhold heaven from someone who is loathsome – but not as a punishment, since, according to this argument, Christ has no original guilt. If this is the case, then Christ cannot be sinless, even if he is not guilty. But then he would not be merely fallen, but fallen and sinful. So, the argument folds once again, for the same reason as before: it is theologically unorthodox.

Third, it is metaphysically impossible for the impeccable divine nature of the Word to be joined in hypostatic union with a fallen human nature as this view proposes. According to classical theology, the Word is incapable of sinning, or being in any way polluted by sin. Yet, on this view, he would be joined with a human nature that is loathsome to the point of being unfit for entry into heaven, and that would implicate him in its vitiated state (in the hypostatic union). God is not implicated in my sinful condition, although he upholds and penetrates every fibre of my being, because he is not *morally* responsible for my sin, though he is responsible for keeping me in existence and enabling me to bring about the sin I commit. The same is not true of the relation between the Word and his human nature, according to the fallenness view, precisely because it is *his* human nature. The Word creates and assumes this human nature; it is 'part' of the Word. So he is morally responsible for it just as, in a similar way, I am morally responsible for the actions of my body that I bring about. Thus, even if it were possible for the Word to assume a fallen human nature in the Incarnation (which it is not, if he is essentially impeccable), he would cease to be impeccable at that moment, which, according to classical theology, is equivalent to saying that he would cease to be a divine being at that moment, because impeccability is an essential divine property. This is intolerable, as well as unorthodox.[29]

What this shows is that, although the motivation that has driven certain Reformed theologians to accept the idea that Christ's human nature is fallen is a laudable one, viz. redeeming our fallen human nature, identifying himself with us in our fallenness, healing our fallen state by taking it upon himself and redeeming it, and so forth, it is misguided and has very seriously damaging theological consequences.

A fourth point drives this concern home. If Christ has a fallen human nature, then it appears that the only way that this can obtain is if we deny Chalcedonian Christology and embrace a version of Nestorianism, according to which the Word is not hypostatically united with his human nature, but lives a sort of parallel existence to it. Only if the Word is not intimately united with this fallen human nature can his impeccability remain intact. But Chalcedonian Christology presumes that the relation between the two natures is one of identity: the Word *is* the Christ. This, however, is simply impossible if Christ has a fallen human nature. Imagine a computer that has software installed, and whose software runs perfectly, without a

---

[29] But might not the Word be able to 'insulate' himself from the effects of a fallen human nature, so that he could assume such a nature in the Incarnation? Perhaps one could argue that the property 'being fallen', like the property 'being finite', belongs only to his human nature and does not necessarily affect the divine nature in any harmful or damaging way. But it is one thing to suggest that the Word can assume a human nature that is finite in power and knowledge; it is quite another to claim that he may assume a human nature that has original corruption and is loathsome in the sight of God.

hitch. We might say there was a harmony between the hardware and the software on this particular computer. This is like the traditional way of thinking about the hypostatic union: two natures existing together harmoniously and in complete accord. But consider the same computer after a virus has been introduced into its software. This particular virus is extremely dangerous, and is able to infect and impair not just the software through which it gained a foothold in the computer, but the hard drive too. In fact, this virus, once introduced, will destroy the proper functioning of the computer, causing irreversible damage. The virus, introduced from the software to the hardware of the computer, is rather like the original corruption of a fallen human nature affecting the divine nature in the hypostatic union. Just as there is an intimate relation between the software and hardware such that the introduction of the virus will affect both, so the two natures of Christ are so intimately related that, if the human nature of Christ were to possess original corruption – even without original guilt – this would affect the divine nature of the Word too. The two-natures doctrine presumes that the relation between the two natures of Christ is far more intimate than that between a computer hard drive and its software. But this only reinforces the point being made here. If the relation between Word and assumed human nature in the Incarnation is more intimate than this – indeed, is a matter of identity – then the Word cannot be united to a fallen human nature.

Might there be a way for defenders of the fallenness view to circumvent the problems this argument raises by endorsing some other argument, where Christ's humanity is fallen but not sinful, the position defenders of the fallenness view are committed to? That is, could defenders of the fallenness view claim that Christ is fallen and not sinful, contrary to our argument for a fallen and originally corrupt Christ? Not if fallenness requires sinfulness. This is the issue upon which the fallenness view stands or falls. Without some way of distinguishing between the two notions which, I have argued, are entailed on this view of fallenness, no sense can be made of this fallenness view.[30] And, since fallenness requires sinfulness of some sort, no sense *can* be made of the fallenness view along these lines. This leaves the option of revising the traditional doctrine of original sin, in some way that is similar to what has been attempted here, or abandoning a Chalcedonian Christology. However, we have shown that the only obvious candidate for a revision of original sin, using original corruption without original guilt, yields a doctrine that is incompatible with Chalcedonian orthodoxy. Hence, defenders of the fallenness view do not appear able to articulate a version of the doctrine that is orthodox, even if they can make sense of original corruption without original guilt.

None of this denies the traditional position of theologians like Augustine, who say that Christ's sinless human nature was affected by the Fall without actually being fallen. Augustine claims that 'God could of course have taken a man to himself from somewhere else . . . not from the race of that Adam who had implicated the human race in his own sin . . . But God judged it better to take a man to himself from the very race that had been conquered, in order through him to conquer the enemy of the human race; to take one however whose conception from a virgin was inaugurated by the spirit not the flesh, by faith not lust.' He goes on, 'What was born, I say, was a man who had not and never would have any sin at all, a man by whom would be reborn all those who were to be set free from sin, who could not themselves be born without sin.'[31]

---

[30] Of course, I might think something entails something else, and be wrong about this. Granted. But this is not the case here. To those who would deny this, I ask: What does it mean to say Christ has a fallen human nature if this is not a human nature that is sinful? This seems about as sensible as saying that one could conceive of a sphere that has a surface that is not curved.

[31] Augustine, *The Trinity*, trans. Edmund Hill (New York: New City Press, 1991), 13.23, pp. 361 and 362 respectively. Weinandy, in his discussion of Augustine, is guilty of selective citations that fail to give the whole sense of what Augustine is saying on this issue. See his *In the Likeness of Sinful Flesh*, pp. 29ff.

From these two citations it is clear that Augustine believed that Christ is sinless and yet possesses a human nature affected by the Fall. And this makes sense of those biblical passages where Christ is tired, weeps and is sad.[32] So, *qua* human, he has the propensity to physical and perhaps to moral weaknesses. But exemplifying the effects of the Fall is not the same as being fallen, the claim we have been analyzing. An example will make this clear. Imagine a regime that could produce in a person the symptoms of measles without that person having the virus. A person undergoes this regime in the interests of science. He has the symptoms of the condition: spots, a high temperature, feverishness and so forth, but does not have the measles. Augustine and other classical theologians maintain that, in a similar way, Christ possessed the symptoms and effects of being sinful in terms of moral and physical weakness, without himself possessing the sinful human nature that gives rise to these effects. In this sense, then, Christ takes on the infirmities of fallen humanity, but did not take on the condition of fallenness.[33]

Thus, the traditional sinlessness view is able to account for the identification of Christ with fallen human creatures without thereby identifying Christ's humanity with a fallen humanity.

Conclusions

In this chapter I have argued that the traditional doctrine of original sin poses a serious problem for defenders of the view that Christ's human nature was fallen, rather than sinless. Although it is possible to construct an argument that avoids this problem by revising the way in which original sin applies to the case of Christ's humanity, this revision has a number of undesirable consequences for the defender

---

[32] To illustrate this from just one of the canonical Gospels, see John 4.6; 11.33, 35.

[33] Professor Paul Helm suggested his thought-experiment to me in private correspondence.

of the fallenness view, and, in any case, appears to be subject to insurmountable difficulties if one wishes to retain a Chalcedonian Christology. If so, the argument cannot be used as a successful defence of the fallenness view.

I have not claimed that there is no other argument that may be mounted in defence of the fallenness view. I do not know whether there is such an argument, only that one potential candidate argument, the argument I have mounted, does not work. And any such candidate argument has to overcome apparently insuperable difficulties posed by this view, difficulties to do with the fact that fallenness requires original sin.

5 | Divine kenosis

To say that the Creative Word was so self-emptied as to have no being except in the infant Jesus, is to assert that for a certain period the history of the world was let loose from the control of the Creative Word.

Archbishop William Temple

Kenotic Christology is the view, drawn from New Testament passages such as Philippians 2.7,[1] that, in becoming incarnate, the second person of the Trinity somehow emptied himself (*ekenosen*) of certain divine attributes in order to become truly human. This view has had a rather chequered history in Christian doctrine, and, at least in the versions current in the literature, seems to be of recent vintage, dating back to the nineteenth century.[2] There are some systematic theologians who are defenders of kenotic Christology today.[3] And in the recent literature, several philosophical theologians have sought to show that a case can be made for the doctrine, which helps in

---

[1] '[Christ] emptied himself [*ekenosen*], [and] took on himself the form of a servant, [and] was made in the likeness of men . . .'

[2] See John Macquarrie, *Jesus Christ in Modern Thought* (London: SCM Press, 1990), ch. 11, and Donald Macleod, *The Person of Christ* (Leicester: Inter-Varsity Press, 1998), ch. 8, both of whom give accounts of the history of the doctrine.

[3] This is the case despite Macquarrie's comment that 'the kenotic christologies, whether German or English, turned out to be no more than an episode in modern thinking about the person of Jesus Christ'. *Jesus Christ in Modern Thought*, p. 250. As we shall see, this is rather wide of the mark. A number of recent philosophical theologians have defended versions of kenotic Christology, and the concept of kenosis has found wider application in current systematic theology. See, for example, John Polkinghorne (ed.), *The Work of Love: Creation as Kenosis* (Grand Rapids: Eerdmans, 2001).

explaining how Christ could be 'fully God and fully man' at one and the same time.[4] In this chapter we shall restrict ourselves to consideration of the recent philosophical-theological literature on the subject, making reference to the wider literature on kenotic Christology only where it is germane to this contemporary discussion of the doctrine.

This chapter approaches the topic of kenotic Christology by outlining two generic versions of the doctrine that are often conflated in the literature. These two sorts of kenotic Christology we shall designate 'ontological' and 'functionalist', respectively. An ontological issue in Christology has to do with the being of Christ, whereas a functionalist issue in Christology is one that emphasizes one or other function that Christ performed. So an ontologically kenotic account of Christology claims that, in the Incarnation, the Word abdicates certain divine properties, perhaps for the duration of the Incarnation, perhaps from the Incarnation onward, at all subsequent moments in time. An alternative, and stronger, ontological kenotic account of the Incarnation involves claiming that, at the Incarnation, the Word relinquishes his divinity altogether, emptying himself out in order to become a man, and then taking his divinity up once again at the ascension. Let us call this the *strong ontological kenotic account of the Incarnation*, or 'strong ontological account' for short. Although this strong ontological account is often touted in the

---

[4] See Thomas V. Morris, *The Logic of God Incarnate* (Ithaca: Cornell University Press, 1986), ch. 4; Richard Sturch, *The Word and The Christ* (Oxford: Oxford University Press, 1991), Excursus 3; Peter Forrest, 'The Incarnation: a philosophical case for kenosis', *Religious Studies* 36 (2000): 127–140; C. Stephen Evans, 'The self-emptying of love: some thoughts on kenotic Christology', in Stephen Davis, Daniel Kendall and Gerald O'Collins (eds.), *The Incarnation* (Oxford: Oxford University Press, 2002), ch. 11; Ronald J. Feenstra, 'Reconsidering kenotic Christology', in Ronald J. Feenstra and Cornelius Plantinga Jr (eds.), *Trinity, Incarnation and Atonement* (Notre Dame: University of Notre Dame Press, 1989); John Hick, *The Metaphor of God Incarnate: Christology in a Pluralistic Age* (Louisville: Westminster John Knox Press, 1993), ch. 6; and Stephen T. Davis, *Logic and The Nature of God* (London: Macmillan, 1983), ch. 8.

literature, very few theologians have adopted it as a serious view.[5] In any case, it is clearly incompatible with Chalcedonian Christology, since it entails that the Word ceases to be a member of the divine Trinity for the period of Incarnation, which is unorthodox. (If – *per impossibile* – the Incarnation involves the Word relinquishing all his divine properties, then he ceases to be divine for the period that he relinquishes those properties.) For this reason alone, I shall not consider this strong ontological account in what follows.[6]

By contrast, a functionalist-kenotic account of Christology defends the much weaker claim that the Incarnation involves the Word not exercising certain divine properties for a period of time, typically (although, as we shall see, not necessarily) the period spanning the virginal conception of Christ to his ascension. In what follows, I will contend that the ontological version of the doctrine is problematic, given a traditional picture of the divine nature, and may not be compatible with Chalcedonian Christology. For if, in becoming incarnate, the Word relinquishes omniscience, say, or omnipotence (both common claims among ontological kenoticists), then in an important sense Christ is not 'one and the same Son, the same perfect in Godhead and the same perfect in manhood, truly God and truly man', as Chalcedon states. The functionalist account is compatible with much more of a traditional doctrine of God, but still requires too much of the traditional understanding of God and

---

[5] Wolfgang Friedrich Gess held to a strong ontological account of kenoticism. See his *Die Lehre von der Person Christi, entwickelt aus dem Selbstbewusstsein Christi und aus dem Zeugniss der Apostel* (Basel: Bahnmaiers Buchhandlung, 1856), pp. 304–305. David Brown's discussion of the matter also sounds like an ontological account; see his *The Divine Trinity* (London: Duckworth, 1985), pp. 256ff.

[6] Donald Macleod and Richard Swinburne each claim that certain sorts of kenotic Christology entail the Word's wholesale abandonment of divinity in the Incarnation. (See Macleod, *The Person of Christ*, p. 205, and Swinburne, *The Christian God* (Oxford: Oxford University Press, 1994), p. 233.) But, as C. Stephen Evans puts it, 'any theory that can be described [as] "God ceasing to be God" or "God relinquishing divinity" will not count as a kenotic theory that is attempting to make Chalcedonian orthodoxy intelligible.' 'The self-emptying of love', p. 248.

the Incarnation to be given up. Withholding the exercise of certain divine attributes for the duration of the Incarnation implies a real change in the Word from his preincarnate to his incarnate state that is monumental.[7] As Donald Macleod observes: 'Supposing Einstein had suddenly been reduced to a mollusc, the shock could not have been greater.'[8] I shall end by suggesting that the language of kenosis in the New Testament can be accounted for on a traditional version of Christology that I shall call *kryptic Christology* (although, as I shall suggest in that section of the chapter, it may turn out that a kryptic account is, given a certain understanding of the relationship between functionalist and krypsis accounts, a species of weak functionalist kenotic doctrine).

Before proceeding, a caveat. Some theologians appear, at times, to count certain Christological positions as kenotic which do not seem to me to be true versions of kenoticism. For instance, Richard Sturch claims that the statement that 'the knowledge and power of Jesus is limited, but not those of God the Son', *might* be an acceptable usage of the term 'kenotic'. But he quickly goes on to say: 'If then, this . . . type of Christology is to be called 'kenotic', then the present

---

[7] Typically, functional kenoticists claim only that *some* of the divine attributes are withheld by the Word during the Incarnation. But it might be thought that the exercise of a given attribute entails withholding other powers the divine nature has. For instance, creating and conserving the world means withholding the power to annihilate the world for that period. But this is to confuse the exercise of a divine attribute with the way in which the attribute is exercised. If God exercises his omnipotence in creating or conserving the world, he cannot, at one and the same-time, annihilate it. Both actions require the exercise of divine omnipotence. But the way in which God exercises his omnipotence in a given situation may differ according to what he wills is the case. I am assuming that the exercise of the divine attributes is compossible (i.e. exercising one attribute does not conflict with, or somehow cancel out the exercise of, another attribute) and that withholding the exercise of a divine attribute includes the various ways in which a given attribute could be exercised in a particular state of affairs. And, with classical theologians, I am assuming that withholding the exercise of a divine attribute involves a real change in the divine nature, incompatible with a traditional account of divine immutability.
[8] Macleod, *The Person of Christ*, p. 210.

work [viz. his monograph on Christology, *The Word and the Christ*], is kenoticist and I should be willing to defend the idea of kenosis. Whether this is really proper from the point of view of vocabulary is another matter; I should doubt it myself.'⁹ On my reading of kenosis, this sort of view would not count as kenotic (although it sounds a little kryptic). It is simply Chalcedonian orthodoxy. Only those views of the Incarnation which state that the Word somehow empties himself of – or abstains from the use of all of the powers of – one or more of his divine attributes, either functionally or ontologically, will count as kenotic theories for the purposes of the argument of this chapter.¹⁰

Two versions of kenotic Christology

Ontological kenosis

The ontological view of kenosis makes the strong claim that Christ actually did not have certain divine properties during his earthly sojourn. That is, the second person of the Trinity relinquished certain divine properties for the duration of the Incarnation, such that he was ignorant, powerless and perhaps even spatially limited to the body of Christ for that period. We shall designate this the *standard ontological account*. As we shall see, there is an even stronger version of ontological kenoticism than this, which states that the Incarnation required the abdication of *certain* divine attributes *per se*. This second sort of ontological account we shall call the *standard-plus ontological account*. (This is not the same as the idea that the Incarnation involved the abdication of *all* divine attributes *per se*. The latter claim – of the strong ontological account – we have already rejected.)

---

⁹ Sturch, *The Word and the Christ: An Essay in Analytic Christology* (Oxford: Oxford University Press, 1991), pp. 255 and 259 respectively.

¹⁰ Swinburne makes a similar point with respect to the Christology of Charles Gore; see *The Christian God*, p. 230 n. 32.

To make the standard ontological account clear, consider the example of the comic-book superhero Superman. If Superman is subjected to the influence of green kryptonite, a radioactive chunk of rock recovered from the destruction of his home planet, Krypton, then he may lose his superhuman powers for a period. Were this to happen, then Superman would actually be unable to exercise any superhuman capacities even if he desired to do so, since, due to the malign influence of the green kryptonite, he would cease to have these powers for a particular period. This means that, either as Superman or as Clark Kent, Superman is unable to act in a superhuman way for that period, since Superman (and, therefore, his alter ego, Clark Kent) has no superhuman powers for the period of his exposure to kryptonite. In a similar fashion, ontological kenotic theories claim that during the period of the Incarnation the second person of the Trinity relinquishes certain properties pertaining to his divinity, such as omnipotence and omniscience, so that, in the Incarnation, the man Jesus of Nazareth is ignorant of certain things and has only a limited amount of power for the period of his life on earth, because the divine Word becomes ignorant of certain things and limited in power for this period, having abdicated the divine prerogatives of omniscience and omnipotence for the duration of the Incarnation.[11]

In the literature, Stephen Davis has given a philosophically interesting account of this standard ontological sort of kenotic theory. His argument takes the following form.

(1) God has certain essential and certain contingent properties.
(2) One contingent divine property is omniscience.
(3) At the Incarnation, the Word assumes a human nature.

---

[11] On this view the abdication of omnipotence is just the abdication of all supernatural power beyond some threshold that mere human beings cannot possess, like Superman's ability to fly. That is, there is some point beyond which divine power is omnipotent, and is relinquished in the Incarnation. Like Superman, Christ has the powers of a human being. The question is whether he also has divine powers during the Incarnation, or not, just as Superman has human powers, but also superhuman powers, even when he is Clark Kent.

(4) For the period of Incarnation, the Word relinquishes certain contingent divine properties, including omniscience.

(5) In the Incarnation, the Word does not relinquish any essential divine properties.[12]

There are two important issues here. One is a general point do with the sort of properties the divine nature has; the other is a more specific contention about the properties relinquished by the Word in the Incarnation (what we might call the ontological-kenosis issue). First, Davis makes the non-traditional theological claim that not all of the properties of the divine nature are essential to the divine nature.[13] On this view, it seems, God has properties that are not part of his essence, which are accidental or contingent, which he could lose or relinquish, while remaining divine. The particular property Davis discusses is omniscience, but presumably there are other such properties, although he does not specify which they may be. The second claim follows upon the heels of the first, so to speak. Davis maintains that, provided the Word retains those properties that are essential for divinity, he may relinquish, or cease to exemplify, those properties that are non-essential for his divinity, for the period of the Incarnation. This means that, during the Incarnation, the Word may give up his omniscience (and, perhaps, other non-essential divine attributes) and remain divine. Thus, Davis:

> Is it true that God would not be God if he were not omniscient, e.g. if he had forgotten some fact? I don't see how anyone could know this. I cannot prove that omniscience is an accidental rather than essential

[12] See Davis, *Logic and the Nature of God*, pp. 124ff.

[13] Classical theologians were united in affirming that all divine properties are essential to the divine nature. For recent discussion of this, see Alvin Plantinga, *Does God Have a Nature?* (Milwaukee: University of Marquette Press, 1980); Jay Wesley Richards, *The Untamed God* (Downers Grove: InterVarsity Press, 2003), ch. 1; and Richard Muller, *Post-Reformation Reformed Dogmatics*, III: *The Divine Essence and Attributes* (Grand Rapids: Baker, 2003).

property of God, but it seems so to me . . . Furthermore, the fact that I believe both that Jesus Christ was God and that Jesus Christ was non-omniscient leads me to deny that omniscience is essential to God.

Moreover,

> This means, I believe, that the Second Person of the Trinity voluntarily and temporarily gave up those properties every divine being has that are inconsistent with being truly human. Thus it is false to say that in the incarnation Jesus Christ had all the divine properties or was God *simpliciter*.[14]

This is a subtle version of ontological kenoticism. By dividing the divine attributes up into those that are essential to divinity and those that are not, and by placing among the contingent divine attributes all those properties which (on an ontological kenotic Christology) the Word must relinquish in order to become human, Davis avoids the obvious problem with ontological kenoticism. That is, he avoids saying that the Word relinquishes certain divine properties *essential* to his divinity, in order to become incarnate. According to Davis, those properties that are relinquished in the Incarnation are not

---

[14] Davis, *Logic and the Nature of God*, p. 124. Unfortunately, Davis obscures his argument when he later claims: 'I believe it is quite possible for an *essentially* omniscient being temporarily to take non-omniscient form and all the while still be the same *essentially* omniscient being' (p. 125, emphasis added.) Clearly this is metaphysically impossible: an essentially omniscient being cannot relinquish his omniscience without also relinquishing his divinity. I take it that Davis means to say something more in keeping with his previous argument, namely, that a *contingently* omniscient being can temporarily take non-omniscient form while remaining a divine being, provided omniscience is not an essential property of divinity. Alternatively, he could be articulating a version of functionalist kenoticism. Then, an essentially omniscient divine being withholds the exercise of his omniscience for a period of Incarnation. But that does not fit with Davis's prior comments about essential and contingent divine properties. I have taken him to be defending a standard ontological account. If I am wrong about this, then his argument is a version of functionalist kenoticism.

essential to divinity; they are contingent properties that a divine person may or may not have. For this reason, the Word may surrender contingent properties like omniscience for the period of the Incarnation, without the Word divesting himself of his divinity at the same time.[15]

But this solves the obvious problem with ontological kenoticism only at the considerable cost of moving away from a traditional account of the divine nature. Davis claims not to be able to see why God cannot have certain properties, like omniscience, contingently. But no classical theologian would concur with him in this matter. A scriptural case can be made for the idea that an unchanging and constant God is one whose character – and properties – do not change.[16] It is this reading of the biblical tradition, along with certain metaphysical commitments, that led classical theologians to claim that the divine nature is *de re* necessary, and that God has no accidental properties, apart from merely relational properties, such as being the creator of Adam at one moment, and the one who curses Adam at another moment.[17] That is, all the properties of the divine nature, including such things as omniscience, omnipotence and omnipresence, are necessary to the divine essence. God cannot exist without

[15] A similar point is made by Ronald J. Feenstra in 'Reconsidering kenotic Christology', p. 135.

[16] My point here is just that one can make a good biblical case for saying that God's character does not change; he is constant (see, e.g. Mal. 3.6; 2 Pet. 3.8). One way of thinking about this is to say that God has certain properties that make up his character, and these properties do not change. So, his character does not change. Alternatively, if God is simple, then his character is incapable of change. These are not the only ways one could read the biblical account, but they are two traditional ways of doing so.

[17] Allowing that classical theology involved certain metaphysical as well as certain theological commitments is not the same as saying that classical theologians had a Procrustean bed of metaphysical ideas upon which they made the teaching of Scripture fit, even if it meant doing violence to that teaching. This Harnackian reading of classical theology is simply false, as well as naïve. For an interesting defence of this traditional view, see Paul Helm's contribution to Gregory E. Ganssle (ed.), *God and Time: Four Views* (Downers Grove: InterVarsity Press, 2001).

exemplifying all these properties.[18] In fact, strictly speaking, theologians like Augustine, Anselm and Aquinas (the 'A' Team of classical theology) claimed that if God is a simple being, without parts, he is incapable of essential change. (These theologians wanted to retain some sort of Trinitarian distinctions in the divine nature, and a strong doctrine of divine simplicity. Quite how this can be achieved is beyond the scope of the present discussion.[19]) In which case, there is no metaphysical possibility of the divine nature changing. If either the view that God has a *de re* necessary nature, or the medieval view that God is simple, is true, then Davis's characterization of the divine nature in terms of contingent and essential properties fails to get off the ground.[20]

Of course, a number of contemporary theologians have argued that the classical view of the divine nature is seriously flawed.[21] If one were to take this sort of line, then whether or not Davis (or some

---

[18] Perhaps the kenoticist will claim that these properties belong to God *simpliciter*, not to God Incarnate. Then, the Father and Spirit retain these properties when the Son relinquishes them at the Incarnation. But this raises two issues. First, this looks *de facto* binitarian. Second, it involves a commitment to Arianism, according to which the Son is not of the same substance as the Father and the Spirit, which is unorthodox.

[19] Richard Muller suggests, *contra* Alvin Plantinga, Nicholas Wolterstorff and others that the medievals did not think of divine simplicity as excluding all distinctions in the divine nature, because they all agreed upon the distinctions requisite for a doctrine of the Trinity. See Muller, *Post-Reformation Dogmatics*, III, pp. 38ff.

[20] See, e.g. Anselm, *Proslogion* 18, and Thomas Aquinas, *Summa Theologiae* 1.3. Feenstra, in defence of Davis, claims that, just as there may be no agreement on the necessary and sufficient conditions for membership of humankind, so there may be no agreement on the necessary and sufficient conditions of divinity. Thus there might be contingent and necessary properties in the divine nature. See Feenstra, 'Reconsidering kenotic Christology', p. 137. But, on arguably the most influential account of the divine nature, namely the Anselmian account, there is widespread agreement on what are great-making properties of divinity. At the very least, there is agreement among classical theologians that God is an immutable, *de re* necessary being who has no intrinsic accidental properties.

[21] For two very different recent accounts of why the traditional doctrine of the divine attributes is flawed, see Colin Gunton, *Act and Being* (Grand Rapids: Eerdmans, 2003), and Plantinga, *Does God Have a Nature?*

other kenoticist) holds a view of the divine nature that is revisionist will not be the article on which his argument stands or falls. We cannot attempt a comprehensive apology for a classical view of the divine nature here. But a few words in defence of the traditional view might be appropriate.

Let us focus on two of the divine attributes, omniscience and immutability, since these two are important for present purposes. First, on the matter of omniscience, if the Word may relinquish this divine attribute for some period of time, this seems to have several unfortunate consequences Davis does not seem to be cognizant of. To begin with, giving up omniscience means, for the period during which he is non-omniscient, that Christ does not know what he does not know. For instance, perhaps ignorance of an infinite number of propositions is entailed by not knowing the hour of the second coming. (Even if ignorance of the hour of the second coming does not entail ignorance of an infinite number of other propositions, it may still entail ignorance of a very sizeable number of propositions.) If Christ gives up his omniscience during the Incarnation, then for that period he cannot know which these propositions are. In fact, he cannot even venture an opinion on which these propositions are, for fear of being mistaken. And this, I venture to suggest, seems to be a very serious problem for a member of the divine Trinity.

Second, regarding immutability: I take it that defenders of the traditional picture of the divine nature will say that divine immutability precludes God from changing his desires or his actions related to those desires, because God's mental life is not like ours in this respect (he has no potentiality). Moreover, on this view, God has only essential attributes, which, if one is a defender of divine simplicity, are predicates we ascribe to God, not properties that God has (he has no composition). But divine simplicity is a contentious matter for many contemporary theologians. So, let us ascribe a version of immutability to God that does not require it, but is compatible with it (if it turns out that God is simple). Then, the divine nature has no accidental properties (here on read 'predicates' if you are a divine-simplicity partisan). He has only essential properties, and these properties do not change. This is consistent with the idea that God may have properties that ascribe merely relational change between God and his creatures that are trivial – what are often called 'merely Cambridge' changes – such as the relation God has to a creature at one moment in one place, and the relation he has to the same creature at the next moment in another place. The 'change' involved here has no important consequences for the divine nature.

Now, it might be thought that God has desires upon which he may or may not act, which would entail change in God, such as seems to be reported immediately prior to the biblical Flood, when God 'repents' of ever having created human beings (Gen. 6.6). It might also be thought that the divine nature has certain properties apart from this that are contingent. The Incarnation of the Word looks like such a property. But classical theology has maintained that God's 'repenting' of certain actions in Scripture is on a par with saying that God has an arm (Isa. 53.1), or that 'the eye of the Lord is on those who fear him' (Ps. 33.18). This is just anthropomorphism, a way in which God accommodates himself to our limitations in revealing himself in Scripture. Such biblical passages do not necessarily imply that God has desires that change, or actions that he regrets.[22] Nor is the Incarnation necessarily a change of the right sort for ontological kenoticists. Classical theologians distinguished between the assumption of human nature in the person of the Word, and assumption of human nature in the divine nature. The former they affirm; the latter they deny. It is not, they argue, that the Incarnation involves a change in the nature of God. What it involves is a relational change between the Word and the human nature he contingently assumes. Much as, we might think, putting on a garment does not mean that

---

[22] Indeed, there are good biblical reasons for thinking that God does not change. See, for example, 'God is not . . . a mortal, that he should change his mind' (Num. 23.19); 'The Glory of Israel will not recant or change his mind' (1 Sam. 15.29); 'The Lord . . . will not change his mind' (Ps. 110.4); 'the Father of lights, with whom there is no variation or shadow due to change' (James 1:17).

I have changed substantially, so, according to one sort of classical Christological argument, the assumption of human nature by the Word does not change the Word substantially, but merely in relation to what is assumed.

All of this would need much fuller explanation if we were engaged in defending the traditional picture of the divine nature. But we are not. I am just trying to sketch out several aspects of the traditional account, in order to show that a case can be made for this particular construal of the divine nature (which ontological kenoticists reject).

In a later account of his kenotic Christology, Davis tries to respond to this sort of criticism.[23] He says that there is a distinction to be made between properties that we might predicate of God *simpliciter*, and properties that we might predicate of a being that is truly divine. The Incarnate Word is truly divine. Yet he seems to lack certain properties that God *simpliciter* has, such as omniscience. Does this mean that the Incarnate Word is not divine because, on this kenotic account, he lacks omniscience? Not necessarily. It could be that a divine being need not have all the same properties as God *simpliciter*. This might be because the Incarnate Word lacks, for a certain period, certain properties that characterize God *simpliciter*. Davis says that this objection to his kenotic theory 'errs in taking supposed properties of God *simpliciter* and then asking whether those properties can be had by God incarnate'.[24] That is, the classical picture of the divine nature has the cart before the horse. We should allow the doctrine of the Incarnation to inform what properties are requirements for the divine nature, rather than stipulating that God must have certain properties and then trying to make this fit with a doctrine of Incarnation. Moreover, a concept of God *simpliciter* that is *prima facie* incompatible with a kenotic theory of Incarnation should be rejected in favour of a kenotic view. Such a picture of God is an unhelpful abstraction;

---

[23] See Davis's contribution to Stephen T. Davis (ed.), *Encountering Jesus: A Debate on Christology* (Atlanta.: John Knox Press, 1988), pp. 54ff.

[24] Ibid., p. 55.

Christians believe in the God who is incarnate in Christ, not some deity whose divine nature has certain properties that preclude his kenotically assuming human nature.[25]

But this argument depends upon a dubious assumption. It is not necessarily the case that classical theologians have a preformed doctrine of God and then struggle to fit a doctrine of Incarnation into this conception of God. Nor is it necessarily the case that a doctrine of Incarnation inevitably ends up with the sort of kenotic theory that Davis advocates. Davis is quite clear that he takes the doctrine of the Incarnation, understood kenotically, as the 'control' for a doctrine of God. Christ is not omniscient. This seems to point to the fact that somehow the Word is not omniscient for the duration of the Incarnation. So omniscience turns out not to be an essential divine property. But why believe this? Why not, with the host of classical theologians who thought about this matter with care and rigour, think that the Word retains his omniscience but that the human nature of Christ is not omniscient?[26] Why not say that, in the hypostatic union, the Word interpenetrates the human nature of Christ, but the converse is not the case, such that the human nature of Christ simply does not have certain properties or predicates that the divine nature of Christ does? This seems to me to be entirely in keeping with the tradition without conceding that the Incarnation involves the Word relinquishing certain divine properties.[27]

---

[25] These last comments about the sort of God Christians believe in is inferred from what Davis actually says. However, C. Stephen Evans also reads Davis in this way in 'The self-emptying love', p. 255.

[26] One reason to deny this: it undercuts the unity of the person of Christ and is incipient Nestorianism. But why should this be the case on something like a two-minds Christology? The human mind is contained in the divine mind, but the converse is not the case. The divine mind has access to everything in the human mind, but the converse is not the case. This is not clearly Nestorian or unorthodox.

[27] Stephen Evans claims that there seems to be a contradiction between Davis's first statement of his kenotic view and the second ('The self-emptying love', p. 255). But I cannot see how the two versions contradict one another. Davis explicitly states that omniscience is not an essential property of God. The difference seems to be one of

There are other problems for Davis's version of ontological kenoticism. For instance, it is very difficult indeed to know where to draw the line demarcating contingent and essential divine properties. For if omniscience turns out to be a contingent rather than an essential divine property, then what are we to make of omnipotence, omnipresence, eternity or benevolence, to name four other divine attributes traditionally thought to be essential to the divine nature? If it is possible for one of the persons of the Godhead to relinquish his knowledge, why can he not relinquish his power, or limit his presence, his eternal life or his goodness? In fact, if omniscience is not an essential property of the divine nature, then omnipotence does not seem to be so either, since to lose omniscience is to lose a power that was previously held. And to lose power looks like a loss of omnipotence. Or take another problem with this view. As we have already seen, God is traditionally thought to be immutable, on biblical and theological as well as philosophical grounds. If he is essentially unchanging, then he cannot gain or lose attributes without also ceasing to be divine. The burden of proof lies with Davis to demonstrate how such a radical revision of the traditional picture of the divine nature is able to distinguish between essential and contingent divine attributes, without undermining the immutability of God (understood in the sense of a being whose properties do not, and cannot, change). One way to present this would be as a slippery-slope argument. Ontological kenoticists who think that certain divine attributes are contingent rather than essential to the divine nature need to show how they can draw a line between these two sorts of attributes that does not seem arbitrary and that prevents them from slipping down the slope of uncertainty about which divine attributes are which.

emphasis, rather than one of substance. Davis also says that his kenotic view is only one way of thinking about the Incarnation (albeit one which he thinks has certain advantages over other views). He is not necessarily committed to saying that kenoticism is the *right* way to think about the Incarnation.

There is one more general problem for ontological kenotic accounts of Christology. If the Word relinquishes certain divine attributes for the duration of Christ's life and ministry, what are we to make of the ongoing life and ministry of Christ after the ascension? For, traditionally, theologians have taught that after his ascension Christ sits at the right hand of the Father, interceding for his saints, and will come again in glory to judge the living and the dead. What is more, Christ will remain fully human as well as fully divine beyond the last judgment, into eternity. He is forever human as well as divine. On the standard ontological kenotic account, the Word temporarily relinquishes certain divine attributes in order to become incarnate. But, on a credally orthodox Christology, there is nothing temporary about the assumption of human flesh by the Word.[28] The Word assumes human nature for ever.[29] In which case, the relinquishing of certain divine properties entailed by the ontological kenotic account is not temporary, but permanent, or everlasting. This seems to pose a serious problem for ontological kenoticism. It is one thing to argue that the Word may relinquish certain properties for a period of time.

---

[28] Ronald Feenstra points out that the definition of Chalcedon states that Christ *is*, not that he *was*, truly human. He also shows that the idea that Christ is forever human is enshrined in the confessions of the Reformation churches. See The Heidelberg Catechism in Philip Schaff (ed.), *Creeds of Christendom*, 4th edn (New York: Harper and Bros., 1877), III, pp. 322–335, questions and answers 46–49 and 78–79; and the Formula of Concord in Theodore G. Tappert (trans. and ed.), *The Book of Concord: The Confessions of the Evangelical Lutheran Church* (Philadelphia: Fortress Press, 1959), art. 7, pp. 568–591, cited in Feenstra, 'Reconsidering kenotic Christology', pp. 147, 152.

[29] Surprisingly few theologians pause to reflect in detail upon this implication of the creed. One who does so is Francis Turretin. He says: 'We maintain that Christ went up locally, visibly and bodily from the earth into the third heaven or seat of the blessed above the visible heavens; not by a mere withdrawal of his visible presence or familiar intercourse, but by a local translation of his human nature. There he will remain until the day of judgement, so that although he is always present with us by his grace and Spirit and divinity, yet he is no longer with us by the bodily presence of his flesh.' *Institutes of Elenctic Theology*, II, trans. George Musgrave Giger, ed. James T. Dennison Jr (Phillipsburg: P&R Publishing Co., 1992), 13.8.3, p. 367. Compare Calvin, *Institutes*, 2.16.14.

It is quite another to claim that the Word relinquishes those properties and will never take them up again from that moment onwards. At the very least, it is not clear how, on such a version of Christology, the Word can be said to remain fully divine after the Incarnation, since, from that moment onwards, there are certain divine attributes that he is forever unable to exercise, having relinquished them at the first moment of Incarnation. This problem of Christ's glorification is not novel. Over half a century ago Donald Baillie asked:

> Was the kenosis merely temporary, confined to the period of the Incarnation of the Son of God, the days of his flesh on earth? The holders of the theory would *logically* have to answer: Yes . . . on the Kenotic theory . . . He is God and Man, not simultaneously in a hypostatic union, but successively – first divine, then human, then God again. But if that is really what the theory amounts to . . . it seems to leave no room at all for the traditional catholic doctrine of the *permanence* of the manhood of Christ.[30]

Some recent defenders of ontological kenoticism have embraced exactly the view that Baillie excoriates.[31] Such a view would count as a standard-plus ontological account of kenosis, that is, a version of kenotic theory where the Word never resumes divine attributes abdicated at the Incarnation. But a defender of ontological kenoticism may claim that this need not follow. The glorified Christ may not suffer the same limitations that the earthly Christ did. In which case, the Word may not be limited by the human nature of the glorified Christ in quite the same way that he was limited in assuming the

---

[30] Donald Baillie, *God Was in Christ* (New York: Charles Scribner's Sons, 1948), p. 97.

[31] One such is David Brown in *The Divine Trinity*, p. 234. Brown claims that Baillie's reasoning in defence of the perpetual humanity of Christ is 'obscure'. It seems clear enough to me: a doctrine that denies the perpetual humanity of Christ is non-catholic. Feenstra makes a good case against Brown in this respect, and I shall not tax the patience of readers by recapitulating what he says in 'Reconsidering kenotic Christology', pp. 144–147.

human nature of the earthly Christ.[32] But then the question naturally arises: In what sense is the glorified Christ less limiting for the Word than the earthly Christ? If Christ is fully human when glorified as he was when on earth, then presumably there will be limitations pertaining to human nature that apply to the glorified as well as to the earthly Christ. Even if the glorified Christ does not suffer all the same limitations in knowledge, power and so forth, that the earthly Christ suffered from, it seems strange indeed to claim that he suffers from none of them and yet remains fully human. It seems to me that an essential property of being human is being limited, at least in some respects, if not all (perhaps not in knowledge or power, for instance, although, as I have argued in chapter one, it would be very strange to think that a human being could be omnipresent). But if that is true, then it is difficult to see how the glorified full humanity of Christ cannot limit the Word in some ways just as the limitations of the earthly Incarnation did. And if this is true, then it is difficult to see how an ontological kenoticist can avoid affirming that, when at the Incarnation the Word relinquished certain divine attributes, including omniscience, he relinquished them for ever, not merely for the period of Christ's earthly existence. What is more, even if the ontological kenoticist can show that Christ may relinquish certain divine attributes for the period of Incarnation only, so that he may take them up once again after his glorification, it is not clear that this means that Christ has these properties essentially at all times post-glorification. If one is able to relinquish certain properties for a period, to then take them up once again at some later time, this would seem to suggest that all such properties are, in fact, accidental or contingent properties, not essential properties, of that thing. But then, Christ is not essentially, that is, omnitemporally, omniscient. He is only contingently omniscient. Or at least, he is contingently omniscient only at those times when he retakes his omniscience, post-glorification

[32] We have already noted, in chapter one, how Lutheran theologians claim that this applies in particular to the ubiquitous nature of Christ's body after his ascension.

135

(that is, this property, like the others he has relinquished for the period of the Incarnation, are not essential to remaining Christ post-glorification). And this seems to be a very unsatisfactory account of the glorified Christ.

On Davis's account, this does not seem to present a problem. After all, on his view, omniscience is not an essential divine attribute. However, even if it is not an essential divine attribute at any time in the life of the Word (before, during, or after the Incarnation), it seems bizarre to say that the Word can relinquish his omniscience from the first moment of Incarnation and at all subsequent moments thereafter. Can a being that is able to relinquish this divine property for merely human-like powers of knowledge from the first moment of Incarnation onwards still be a divine being?

The problem of Christ's glorification can also be taken in a different direction. Assume that the defender of some version of standard ontological kenosis is happy to affirm that the Word abdicates certain divine properties only for the Incarnation prior to Christ's receiving a glorified human body at the resurrection. Thereafter, because he has a glorified body, the limitations placed upon the Word in the Incarnation may not apply. Such a glorified body may have the properties of omniscience and omnipotence. Assume that Christ's glorified body has these properties. Then the question is: If Christ's glorified body has omnipotence and omniscience, why is it that his pre-resurrection human nature may not also have these properties? What is it about the pre-resurrection humanity of Christ that requires the Word to relinquish the divine properties he does relinquish, in order to become Incarnate? Some reason would need to be given to explain why it is that the pre-resurrection Christ may not possess omnipotence or omniscience, whereas the post-resurrection Christ (with a glorified body) may do so.[33]

---

[33] This is aside from the paradoxical nature of claiming that a being can lay aside its omnipotence or omniscience and be lacking divine power or knowledge for a period, only to take them up at some later time. How can a person divest himself of divine power or knowledge so that he is without these properties, and then decide he will

A response to this argument may be made along the following lines. There is an important difference between the pre- and post-resurrection humanity of Christ. The pre-resurrection humanity of Christ still suffers from the effects of the Fall. He is weak, needs sustenance, suffers and so forth. The post-resurrection Christ does not. One important theme of the Gospel accounts is to show that Christ overcomes death and sin in his body at the cross. The resurrection is that event which inaugurates the glorification of human nature in the person of Christ, as the apostle Paul calls it (1 Cor. 15). Therefore, it seems perfectly reasonable to say that the pre-resurrection human nature of Christ has certain limitations that the post-resurrection human nature does not. And perhaps being non-omniscient and being non-omnipotent are two such limitations that do not figure in the post-resurrection human nature that Christ has. Nevertheless, the post-resurrection human nature of Christ still has limitations in virtue of being embodied. Astute defenders of a standard ontological kenosis account of the Incarnation will have factored this into their exposition of divine kenosis. After all, theologians who defend this view need not be committed to the claim that the Word relinquishes his omnipresence, as well as his omnipotence or omniscience, during the period of Incarnation. Ontological kenosis does seem to require the abdication of properties like omniscience and omnipotence because the Gospels record Christ's ignorance (of some things) and limited power. But in versions other than the strong version, ontological kenosis does not require the abdication of all the divine attributes in the Incarnation. Perhaps omnipresence is an attribute retained by the Word. In which case, such limitations can be accounted for on a version of ontological kenosis.

A final thought on ontological kenosis. A defender of a version of this view might mount the following sort of argument. The

take them up again? This makes as much sense as saying the Queen may abdicate the throne, but only for a period of a few years, whereupon she will ascend the throne once again.

Incarnation is a phase in the life of the Word. (It may even be a necessary phase in the life of the Word, but I shall leave that to one side.) 'Prior' to this phase in his life, the Word has certain essential properties. But during the current phase of his life, the phase of Incarnation, he has a different set of essential properties, some of which overlap with the first set (e.g 'being a person', 'being Christ'), but some of which do not (e.g. 'being limited in power and knowledge'). Perhaps there are certain divine attributes that are what we might call *phase-essential* to the Word, that is, essential to a certain phase of the life of the Word, rather as a tadpole may have certain essential properties a frog does not. Essential to a properly functioning tadpole are things like having a tail and having gills, being herbivorous, and so forth. But essential to a properly functioning adult frog are things like having no tail, having lungs, and, in most species, being carnivorous. These are things that are not essential to being a tadpole, but are essential to being a frog. So it seems there are properties the frog has at a certain stage of its life that are essential to that stage, but not to the whole life of the frog. In a similar way, perhaps there are phase-essential properties that are had by the Word prior to the Incarnation, and another set of phase-essential properties that are had during the Incarnation, though both phases are phases of the life of the Word.

But this sort of reasoning assumes there are phase-essential properties a being might possess that are not necessarily essential to that being, *simpliciter*. In other words, there are things essential to certain phases of the life of an entity that may not be essential to the existence of that entity at all stages of its life. But this does not apply in the case of the Incarnation (according to classical theology, at least). The Word does not have certain divine properties that are only essential to his pre-incarnate phase of existence, but not essential to his incarnate phase of existence. Nor, to put it in terms that parallel our tadpole–frog example, is it the case that the Word has certain properties that he cannot have as a human being, just as the tadpole has certain properties the frog cannot. What happens at the Incarnation is that the Word takes on certain properties *in addition* to his essential divine properties. He does not *relinquish* one set of phase-essential properties in order to take up another set of phase-essential properties. He is a *de re* necessary being who has all his properties essentially. In fact, this sort of manouevre will work only if the theologian is willing to concede to the ontological kenoticist the very point at issue, namely, that there are divine attributes, non-essential to the divine nature, that may only be phase-essential to a particular stage of the life of the Word. But no classical theologian will accept this. And there are good reasons for not accepting this sort of thinking. For one thing, on this view, a divine being can be ignorant of vast numbers of things and powerless to do many different logically possible things for periods of time because omniscience and omnipotence are only phase-essential properties. But this is as implausible as the Einstein-mollusc referred to earlier. Is it plausible to think that Einstein could have certain phase-essential properties as a human being, but exchange these for a different set of phase-essential properties because in some later phase of his life he is reduced to a mollusc? Yet this is what this argument for a version of the ontological kenosis requires in the Incarnation.

I think the problems for the ontological kenosis accounts we have considered are serious and debilitating. There may be aspects of the glorification problem that are also problematic on this version of kenosis, depending on which divine attributes are relinquished in the Incarnation. For these reasons, it seems to me that ontological kenotic accounts of the Incarnation should be abandoned in favour of some weaker understanding of the divine self-emptying.

Functionalist kenosis

The alternative kenotic account is the functionalist one. There are, as we shall see, several strengths of functional kenoticism, as there are several strengths to ontological kenoticism. But let us begin by examining the most straightforward variety of the kenotic account of the Incarnation. A functionalist kenotic theory affirms that, in becoming incarnate, the second person of the Trinity did not abdicate any of his responsibilities or attributes, but merely restricted the exercise of certain of his attributes, such as his power and knowledge, for the period he was incarnate. On this view, the divine nature of Christ retained its omnipotence, omniscience, omnipresence and so forth, but the second person of the Trinity ensured that he did not exercise any of these attributes for the duration of the Incarnation. This, defenders of this view maintain, helps to explain Christ's apparent ignorance of certain things, such as the date of the second coming (e.g. Matt. 24.36), or his limitations as a human being (e.g. Luke 4.2). Although he could have acted in an omnipotent or omniscient way by exercising these divine attributes, he refrained from doing so.

This seems to be somewhat similar to the case of Superman, mentioned earlier.[34] Superman also has a 'human' alter ego, the mild-mannered news reporter Clark Kent. When Superman is in the guise of Kent, it is important that he does not exercise his superhuman powers in order to hide his secret identity. However, Superman, when acting as a superhero, does exercise these powers in the cause of 'truth, justice and the American way'. A similar view of the restrictions the second person of the Trinity places upon himself can be found in the functionalist version of kenotic theory. The Word, like Superman, has certain essential attributes that he exercises as a divine being, which he does not exercise when incarnate in Christ. In this respect, the person of Christ is rather like the guise of Clark Kent.[35] This means

---

[34] The point being made here is similar in tone to Kierkegaard's parable of the King and the Maiden, in *The Parables of Kierkegaard*, trans. W. Lowrie, ed. Thomas C. Oden (Princeton: Princeton University Press, 1978), pp. 40–45.

[35] Were this to be more than a means of illustrating a central aspect of the functionalist account of kenosis, we would need to register some very important qualifications to this sketched comparison between Superman/Kent and the Word/Christ. Not least among these is the fact that Christ is not merely a 'disguise' for the Word of God, as Kent is for Superman. That is the heresy of Apollinarianism. But, since the point is merely to illustrate the way in which, on a functionalist kenoticism, the Word of God withholds his power to exercise powers he has while incarnate, we shall not go into these problems any further here.

that this functionalist account of kenosis is compatible with a classical Christology. For, on this view, the Incarnation does not mean that the second person of the Trinity abdicates any of his essential divine properties in order to become incarnate, but merely that he refrains from exercising those properties during his earthly existence.

Peter Forrest, in a recent article on kenotic theory, maintains that such a functionalist view of kenotic Christology is, in reality, merely a 'quasi-kenotic version of the classical account' of Christology.[36] However, it does not seem to me that the functionalist kenotic theory is the same as a classical account of Christology, since a classical account requires that the second person of the Trinity retains and *exercises* all his essential divine attributes while incarnate, the very thing that functionalist kenoticism denies.[37] Compare, for instance, the Roman Catholic theologian Gerald O'Collins in this regard:

> In its prudent teaching about the Son of God assuming the human condition, the Council of Chalcedon declared that the properties or essential features of both the divine and the human nature are preserved in the incarnation . . . This teaching seems to rule out even a cautious form of kenotic theory, which proposes that the divine properties were, at least temporarily, not preserved after the incarnation, or at least not preserved in action.[38]

It is precisely this notion of the exercise of divine properties that is at issue in the functionalist kenotic account. It is true that the

---

[36] Peter Forrest makes this point in 'The Incarnation: a philosophical case for kenosis'. He prefers the term 'quasi-kenotic' for this view, because it seems to be a version of classical Christology, not a Christology distinct from that family of views. I prefer the designation 'functionalist', since it pertains to the function Christ performs and the way in which the second person of the Trinity voluntarily restricts himself for the period of his Incarnation.

[37] As we shall see, the krypsis account may be a species of weak functionalist kenoticism that avoids this peril.

[38] Gerald O'Collins, *The Incarnation* (London: Continuum, 2002), pp. 62–63. Perhaps a weak functionalist account might be able to overcome this problem. I shall deal with this point in the section on kryptic Christology, below.

functionalist kenotic theory does not require that the second person of the Trinity give up one or more essential divine attributes in order to become incarnate. In this important respect, functional kenoticism is, as Forrest remarks, compatible with the classical Christology. However, what differentiates the classical Christology from functionalist kenotic forms of Christology is more than the fact that the second person of the Trinity retains all his essential divine attributes during the period of Incarnation. It also requires that these divine attributes be exercised throughout the period of Incarnation.

This difference is encapsulated in a theological safeguard to (one version of) the classical Christology, which makes this point clear. This is the so-called *extra calvinisticum*.[39] The *extra calvinisticum* states that while the second person of the Trinity was incarnate in the person of Christ, he was simultaneously providentially sustaining the cosmos. In fact, one of the main reasons for formulating the *extra calvinisticum* was to express the idea that these attributes had to be exercised by the Word in order that the second person of the Trinity (a) remain divine and (b) retain his divine role of upholding the cosmos in being while incarnate. As J. N. D. Kelly observes, with reference to Cyril of Alexandria's Christology:

> The Logos, as he [Cyril] liked to say, 'remains what He was'; what happened was that at the incarnation, while continuing to exist eternally in the form of God, He added to that by taking the form of a servant. Both before and after the incarnation He was the same Person, unchanged in His essential deity. The only difference was that He Who had existed 'outside flesh' (*asarkos*) now became 'embodied' (*ensômatos*).[40]

---

[39] As Paul Helm has recently pointed out (following E. David Willis's *Calvin's Catholic Christology* (Leiden: E. J. Brill, 1966)), the term *extra calvinisticum* is a misnomer. The idea did not originate with Calvin, and can be found in a number of the Fathers. See Paul Helm, *John Calvin's Ideas* (Oxford: Oxford University Press, 2004), ch. 3.

[40] J. N. D. Kelly, *Early Christian Doctrines*, 3rd edn (London: Adam and Charles Black, 1965), p. 319.

We have already seen that the defender of functionalist Christology denies precisely the point at issue in the *extra calvinisticum*, to wit, that the Word has to continue to exercise his divine power in order to uphold the cosmos and retain his status as divine. But this means that the functionalist kenotic account differs in an important respect from at least one influential aspect of the classical Christological view. In which case, it is not obvious that a functionalist kenotic theory is a full-blooded version of classical Christology, as Forrest maintains. In fact, if, as it seems, a version of the classical account has to take into consideration the ongoing activity of the second person of the Trinity in the providential upholding of the cosmos during the Incarnation, it is very difficult to see how a functionalist kenotic theory could be a version of a classical account of Christology, despite the fact that the two views are ontologically equivalent in their retention of all the essential divine attributes in the person of the Word of God during the Incarnation (unlike ontological kenoticism).[41]

To illustrate this point, consider the following example. I take it that defenders of the functionalist kenotic theory claim that Christ's divine nature retained the property of omnipotence, but simply did not exercise it during the Incarnation. However, this option is not open to the defender of a classical Christology. On this view, Christ had the property of omnipotence, or, more precisely, his divine nature had that property, and continued to exercise it during the Incarnation. The reason this does not involve a violation of his humanity (since, it seems, a property of human beings this side of the grave is that they are limited in power) is that omnipotence remained a property of the divine nature alone, and was not shared with the human nature of Christ. That is, the second person of the Trinity retained and exercised his omnipotence during the Incarnation, but the human nature of Christ did not have access to this property and, as a result, did not exercise it.

---

[41] Some kenoticists do affirm the *extra calvinisticum*. But this does not seem entirely consistent with their other claims about the divine nature, unless their kenoticism is something like a krypsis account.

As Thomas Morris has shown, this need not mean that Christ *could* not have exercised the omnipotence of the divine nature, only that he *did* not. It might be that the Word ordained that he would not act in an omnipotent fashion in the person of Christ for the period of the Incarnation, although he might have done. But this need not entail that the Word did not act omnipotently during the Incarnation, provided he did not do so through the human nature of Christ. We might say that there are certain things that the Word does *qua* second person of the Trinity that he does not do *qua* human being. But this is not to say that those things he does not do *qua* human he could not have done *qua* human, had he chosen to do so (I shall return to this point in discussing kryptic Christology).[42]

Stephen Evans has given a kenotic account of Christology that, at certain points, sounds distinctly functionalist (although, it should be said, at other times it sounds distinctly ontological).[43] Taking up an argument found in Richard Swinburne's work, he claims that omnipotence might be a property that entails its own limitation.[44] An omnipotent being, on this view, has to be able to limit the exercise of its power in order to count as omnipotent. A similar account of omniscience and perhaps other divine attributes relevant to a kenotic account of Christology could be given. Then, the Word *qua* second

---

[42] It may also be that, *qua* human, Christ was unaware of the fact that his divine nature was omnipotent; in which case, the ignorance of his human nature about the extent of his divine power would have been another way in which Christ *qua* human being might have been unable to exercise divine power. I take it that the exercise of a divine power requires the intention to exercise that power. So a person who is ignorant of possessing divine power is not in a position to exercise that power. I say this tentatively. Nothing in the argument above depends on this being true.

[43] Part of the problem with the literature on kenotic Christology is that defenders of the doctrine are not always as clear as they might be about whether they are defending an ontological or a merely functional account of the doctrine.

[44] See Evans, 'The self-emptying love', pp. 260ff. He is taking up Swinburne's discussion of omnipotence in *The Coherence of Theism*, rev. edn (Oxford: Oxford University Press, 1994), pp. 157–158.

person of the Trinity has all these traditional divine attributes. But, for the purposes of the Incarnation, he restricts his power, knowledge and so forth. Unlike the ontological account of kenoticism, it is not that the Word *abdicates* or *surrenders* certain of his divine properties in the Incarnation. He retains these properties, but he does not exercise them for the duration of the Incarnation.[45]

Another recent account of kenotic-theory Christology that has a functionalist aspect is that given by Thomas Morris. 'What would be claimed', Morris suggests, 'is that it is not precisely *omniscience* which is a requisite of deity. It is rather a distinct property, the property of being omniscient-unless-freely-and-temporarily-choosing-to-be-otherwise, which is a logically necessary condition of deity.'[46]

Then, a functionalist kenotic Christology could be rephrased accordingly: 'The persons of the Godhead together possess the property of being omniscient-unless-freely-and-temporarily-choosing-to-be-otherwise.' This is an essential property of divinity. And it is a property that allows for exactly what the functional kenoticist claims happens at the Incarnation. The Word relinquishes his omniscience while incarnate. The ingenious thing about this non-standard analysis of omniscience is that it means that the Word can surrender the exercise of his omniscience and remain divine. There is still a distinction between essential and contingent properties in the divine nature here. What is 'essential' is the ability to withhold full exercise of these properties. What is 'contingent' is the actual exercise of the properties. So, the Father and Spirit may have omniscience in

---

45 This sounds similar to the medieval distinction between the absolute and the ordained power of God. It could be, on a functionalist kenotic account, that, according to the absolute power of God, Christ is omnipotent, omniscient and so forth; but, according to the ordained power of God, Christ does not exercise his omnipotence, omniscience and so on while incarnate. But I shall not pursue this way of understanding functionalist kenosis here. A good recent discussion of the absolute and the ordained power of God can be found in Helm, *John Calvin's Ideas*, ch. 11.

46 Morris, *The Logic of God Incarnate*, p. 99.

both the essential and contingent sense, while the Son has it in the essential sense, but not the contingent sense, at least for the period of Incarnation.

But the Morris-type analysis of omniscience, as well as Evans's account (or that part of it which is functionalist), is still open to serious objection from a traditional picture of God as an *immutable* perfect being. (I am laying aside the fact that, if divine simplicity is true, both the Evans and the Morris views are false, simply because God has no properties.) Both the Morris-type analysis and the Evans account mean that the idea of mutability is built into the nature of God. The Word may freely and temporarily give up his knowledge.[47] However, this is inconceivable on a traditional perfect-being theology. On such a view, God is essentially immutable. What is more, his nature (if he has a nature as such) is *de re* necessary. Although it might be possible to show that a being whose nature cannot change in essence may yet have an essential property which admits of certain sorts of change (without a change of essential properties, say), this will not work in the case of God. The traditional picture of God as essentially immutable does not seem to allow for this (even if a certain understanding of a *de re* divine nature does – which I doubt).[48]

So, it seems that functional kenoticists, like ontological kenoticists, must give up an important constituent of a traditional view of the divine nature, namely a strong view of divine immutability. Even if a Morris-type analysis of properties like omniscience is given in order to retain the essential nature of those properties, this involves

[47] In fact, on the view that I have stated, God could give up his knowledge for a temporary period. Clearly, this is too strong: Morris does not want to show that *God* can give up his knowledge for a period, only that one of the persons of the Godhead can. But I think that the relevant adjustment can be made to Morris's notion of omniscience that restricts the deployment of limited knowledge to one, and only one, person of the Godhead, strictly for the purposes of redemption. For discussion of this point, see Forrest, 'The Incarnation: a philosophical case for kenosis', pp. 130–133, and Feenstra, 'Reconsidering kenotic Christology', p. 140.

[48] Morris makes exactly this point against kenotic theories in *The Logic of God Incarnate*, ch. 4. This is one of the major reasons he gives for not endorsing kenotic Christology.

surrendering one important aspect of a traditional picture of the divine nature. Either way, the price for such a kenotic theory seems extremely high.

Moreover, it may be that, on certain versions of the functionalist account of kenosis, a version of the problem of Christ's glorification obtains. We could phrase this in the form of a question: Does the Word restrict the exercise of certain divine attributes just for the period of Incarnation on earth, or does this restriction continue post-resurrection? An answer to this problem would need to address the sorts of difficulties raised earlier, with the relevant adjustments having been made for kenotic account. One aspect of the glorification problem that does appear particularly relevant to the functionalist account is the issue of properties pre- and post-resurrection. Assume that a functionalist account is given where, post-resurrection, the Word removes the restrictions upon the exercise of those divine properties he had withheld in the pre-resurrection incarnate state. Then, it seems, the Word could have functioned *qua* incarnate in a way that does not require his placing restrictions upon the exercise of those properties which he exercises post-resurrection. But here, as before in discussing this problem with respect to ontological kenosis, the kenotic theologian could take the view that there are important theological and metaphysical reasons why the Word restricts himself pre-resurrection in a way that he does not do post-resurrection. And this seems to me to be right. In which case, although there are problems for functionalist kenotic Christology, this is not necessarily one of them.

Divine krypsis

Not all accounts of divine self-emptying are kenotic accounts of Christology. Or, to put it less enigmatically, an understanding of the New Testament's witness to some sort of self-emptying in the Incarnation need not entail one or other of the kenotic theories we have discussed thus far in this chapter. Divine self-emptying could be taken to mean something other than ontological or functionalist kenoticism. As Swinburne observes, kenotic theories of Christology (in the technical sense of kenotic theories) all have to do with application to a self-emptying in the Incarnation that involves a 'giving up'. However, 'Chalcedon, by contrast, affirms that the humility involves a taking on. The king humbles himself by becoming a servant as well as being a king.'[49] This is surely correct. It is not that at the Incarnation the Word empties himself of his divinity in some sense, in order to become human. It is rather that at the Incarnation the Word takes on, in addition to his divinity, a human nature. This divine act is an act of condescension: the second person of the Trinity deigns to take on human nature in addition to his divine nature, for the redemption of his people. And he does so, not just for the period of Jesus' earthly life, but from the first moment of Incarnation, for evermore (although Swinburne would not concur with this last point). The Word is *forever* hypostatically united to the human nature of Christ. But in what sense can we speak of divine self-emptying if not in terms of the theories we have canvassed thus far? In this last section of the chapter, I want to suggest that a traditional, Chalcedonian Christology can account for what kenotic theories of Christology are getting at without the problems associated with the ontological or functionalist theories we have examined. In deference to tradition, I shall call this version of divine self-emptying *divine krypsis*, or divine self-concealment. The two recent treatments of kenotic theory given by John Hick and Donald Macleod have both alluded to this sort of argument, without fleshing it out in detail.[50]

It seems to me that those New Testament passages that affirm the divine kenosis, most notably Philippians 2.7, should not be taken to

---

[49] Swinburne, *The Christian God*, p. 233.

[50] See Hick, *The Metaphor of God Incarnate*, ch. 6, and Macleod, *The Person of Christ*. For the historical development of the Lutheran krypsis Christology – which is different in detail from what is presented here – see Francis Pieper, *Christian Dogmatics*, II (St Louis: Concordia, 1951), pp. 296ff.

express some literal metaphysical fact of the matter (as if the Word literally *empties* himself of his divinity in becoming incarnate).[51] Rather, such passages give us a picture of a deep mystery in the Incarnation: that the Word somehow became human in the Incarnation, without thereby relinquishing his divinity. As Karl Barth put it, 'The kenosis of the Son in the incarnation is not that he wholly or partially ceases to be the eternal Son of the Father (otherwise the incarnation would not be a revelation) but that as the Son of God he is also made the Son of Man.'[52] The way we can make sense of both a divine self-emptying consistent with the New Testament witness, and yet retain a traditional Chalcedonian Christology, depends upon distinguishing between the limitations placed upon the human nature of Christ for the duration of the Incarnation, and the relation this human nature bears to the limitless divine nature of the Word.

To elaborate: in the Incarnation, the Word assumes human nature. He does not in any way abdicate or relinquish any of his divine prerogatives or properties, either temporarily or permanently, in this action. At every moment at which the Word is incarnate, he is also exercising his divine attributes to the full, as he was before the Incarnation. What changes at the Incarnation is the taking on of a human nature in addition to the divine nature of the Word. His human nature, as with other human natures that exist post-Fall, has the properties of being limited in power and ignorant of various things.[53] The divine nature of Christ has no such restrictive properties. In virtue of the omnipresence of the divine nature the Word interpenetrates and indwells the human nature of Christ, but

---

[51] Other New Testament passages that might support a kenotic theory include Mark 13.31–32; Luke 2.52; John 11.23; Acts 10.38; 2 Cor. 8.9; and Heb. 5.7–9.

[52] Karl Barth, *The Göttingen Dogmatics: Instruction in the Christian Religion*, I, ed. Hannelotte Reiffen, trans. Geoffrey W. Bromiley (Grand Rapids: Eerdmans, 1991), p. 156.

[53] It seems that there is biblical evidence for Christ's sharing in these limitations. But it may be that the glorified Christ is both omniscient and omnipotent; in which case being ignorant or limited in power cannot be essential properties of being human.

the converse is not the case. That is, the human nature of Christ retains those properties which express the limitations of the knowledge, power, etc., of his human nature, while being indwelt by the divine nature of the Word. But Christ's humanity is in an intimate, perichoretic relation with the Word, which, as I suggested in chapter one, is of a degree of intimacy not enjoyed by other creatures who are also interpenetrated by the divine nature in some fashion. Thus we have a picture of the hypostatic union wherein the humanity of Christ is indwelt by the divine nature but is necessarily not privy to all that the divine nature is (at least, prior to his glorification).[54]

The important thing to notice in this krypsis account of the hypostatic union is that there are:

(1) a restriction of the exercise of the divine attributes through the human nature of Christ for the period between the virgin conception and death of Christ.

(2) no restriction on the exercise of the divine attributes of the Word in abstraction from the Incarnation (as per the *extra calvinisticum*). And, once resurrected, it may be that Christ has certain properties, like omniscience, that he did not have prior to that time.

But, during the period of his earthly ministry (at least some of) these divine properties are not accessible to the human nature of Christ. Either he is ignorant of possessing them in the hypostatic union, or he does not have access to them *per se*, for the period of earthly

---

[54] This sort of krypsis account seems compatible with Morris's two-minds Christology, and, in particular, with his notion of the asymmetrical accessing relation that exists between the divine mind and the human mind of Christ. See *The Logic of God Incarnate*, p. 103. According to Morris, the divine mind contains the human mind and has immediate access to all that the human mind of Christ does. But the human mind of Christ does not have access to all that the divine mind does. The krypsis account need not be taken as a version of a two-minds Christology, although it does entail a two-natures doctrine.

Incarnation. So there is a sense in which, on the view I have been outlining here, at least some of the properties of the divine nature of Christ are withheld from his human nature. But this does not entail that the divine nature of Christ is restricted in the exercise of his divine attributes. All this means is that he places a restriction upon the access the human nature of Christ has to (at least some of) his divine attributes. This krypsis Christology preserves what is required by a full-blooded Chalcedonianism: the Word does not relinquish or abdicate any of his divine attributes for the period of the earthly Incarnation. And it also makes sense of the notion of self-emptying that is alluded to in the New Testament: the human nature taken on by the Word in the Incarnation is limited and does not have access to those divine properties which the Word exercises, but which would be problematic if possessed by a human being, such as omniscience. The self-emptying is, therefore, a picture of the way in which the Word restricts the exercise of his divine attributes through the person of Christ, and the way in which the human nature of Christ is in an asymmetrical accessing relation with the Word in the hypostatic union. But, importantly, there is no kenosis involved here. The Word does not relinquish or abdicate properties for the purposes of Incarnation. Nor does he withhold the exercise of these properties, except in so far as the human nature of Christ does not exercise these properties.

But, it might be asked, is this not just a version of functional kenotic Christology? There is still, on this krypsis view, a functional change at the Incarnation. The Word restricts the exercise of (certain) divine properties in the person of Christ by restricting the access the human nature of Christ has to these divine properties. And this looks like a weak functionalist kenosis.

However, there is a crucial difference between the functionalist kenotic theories I have considered and the krypsis view. It is this: on functional kenosis views, the Word actually restricts the exercise of his divine attributes *per se*. That is, he restricts the exercise of (certain of) his divine attributes *in toto*, for the period of the earthly Incarnation of Christ. He is not exercising his omnipotence everywhere except in the person of Christ; he is not exercising his omnipotence *at all* during the Incarnation. But, on the krypsis view, the only change to the exercise of the divine attributes of the Word during the Incarnation is in the human nature of Christ. It is only the human nature, in hypostatic union with the Word, which does not have access to (certain) divine attributes. So the restriction the Word places upon the exercise of his attributes is, on this krypsis view, really no restriction on the Word as such. Strictly speaking, it is just that the human nature of Christ taken up in the Incarnation is created such that, for the period of earthly incarnation (or, perhaps for the period of having a non-glorified body), the human nature of Christ has no access to those divine properties that would compromise, or threaten to compromise, the unglorified human nature of Christ. Thus, there is an important difference between the functionalist kenotic account and the krypsis account of the Incarnation.

Even if a functionalist kenotic Christologist maintains that the Word does not restrict the exercise of his divine attributes except in the person of Christ, there is still a difference between the functionalist kenosis account and the krypsis account. The difference is that the krypsis account only declares that the Word restricts the access to divine attributes the human nature of Christ has during the Incarnation. The functionalist kenosis account declares that, minimally, the Word restricts the use of his divine properties in the Incarnation. (Thus, the Word restricts the use of (certain) divine properties in both his divine and human natures during the Incarnation.) If the functionalist kenoticist concedes that this minimal functionalist account is equivalent to a krypsis account, then it seems that there is nothing separating some versions of functionalist kenosis from krypsis, and krypsis becomes one sort of functionalist kenotic account, what we might call the minimalist functional kenosis account.

However, it seems to me that all the functionalist kenosis Christologists I have read want to say something more than this. They want to say that the Word restricts his divine properties in such a way that, in the person of Christ, the Word is not omniscient, omnipotent and so forth. He restricts the exercise of his divine properties, or has Morris-style non-standard divine properties that enable him to simulate the abandonment of certain divine properties for the Incarnation, while actually retaining them. The krypsis account is clear that no restriction is placed upon the Word in the exercise of his properties in the Incarnation. There is only a restriction placed upon the human nature of Christ at the creation of that human nature, which prevents it from accessing these divine attributes in the Incarnation. The functionalist kenotic accounts we have considered are not clear about this, and seem to require more than this. For this reason, it seems to me that there is a distinction to be made between functionalist kenotic (at least, the version of this view we have considered) and krypsis accounts of the Incarnation. (This also shows that a krypsis account of the Incarnation does not require the abandonment of a doctrine of divine immutability. The krypsis account need not involve substantive change in the exercise of the properties of the Word.[55])

This, it seems to me, preserves what is important in the New Testament account of the divine self-emptying, while doing justice to the traditional, Chalcedonian understanding of the Incarnation too. Thus a krypsis Christology succeeds where kenotic Christology fails.

---

[55] Is this krypsis account compatible with divine simplicity or a pure act account of the divine nature? One construal of *actus purus* is that God *ad intra*, or in himself, is pure act – without any unrealized possibilities – but *ad extra*, or in relation to his created order, he is not. This appears commensurate with a krypsis Christology. Divine simplicity is more difficult to make sense of in this context, as in many others. But, as has already been mentioned, not all historical theologians are convinced that in classical theology divine simplicity excludes all distinctions in the divine nature, including distinct predicates. See, for example, Muller, *Post-Reformation Reformed Dogmatics*, III.

6 | Non-incarnational Christology

The situation would surely have been hopeless had the very majesty of God not descended to us, since it was not in our power to ascend to him.

John Calvin

In this final chapter, I want to consider one leading account of Christology that is an alternative to Chalcedon. Whereas defenders of a Chalcedonian approach to Christology all affirm that Jesus of Nazareth was God Incarnate, this alternative way of conceiving Christology maintains that Christ was merely a human being. He was not, in addition to this, a divine being. Following Brian Hebblethwaite, I shall call Christologies that deny this crucial constituent of the Chalcedonian view 'non-incarnational Christologies'.[1]

Perhaps the most important leading exponent of such a view among philosophical theologians is John Hick. Earlier in his career, Hick was instrumental in bringing together the contributors to the symposium *The Myth of God Incarnate*, which, in the late 1970s, set the agenda for non-incarnational accounts of Christology in contemporary philosophical theology.[2] Latterly, as Hick has developed his distinctive approach to religious pluralism, he has returned

---

[1] See Brian Hebblethwaite, *The Incarnation: Collected Essays in Christology* (Cambridge: Cambridge University Press, 1987), passim.

[2] See John Hick (ed.), *The Myth of God Incarnate* (London: SCM Press, 1976). These non-incarnational accounts of Christology given by the 'mythologists', as they became known, did not introduce any new idea into theology that had not already been discussed as far back as Strauss's *The Life of Jesus Critically Examined* in 1846 (ed. Peter C. Hodgson; London: SCM Press, 1973). What was novel about the discussion was the

to Christology in his monograph *The Metaphor of God Incarnate: Christology in a Pluralistic Age.*[3] Since Hick has been such an influential voice in this discussion, I shall consider his views in particular in what follows. In the course of his long career, Hick's Christology has changed from a version of Chalcedonian orthodoxy to his current notion of Incarnation as metaphor. It is his mature views that will be the focus of this chapter.[4] We shall see that, although Hick offers a clear account of Christology without Incarnation, there are several serious problems with his account. What is more, the Christology Hick offers is, in the final analysis, religiously inadequate as a Christian account of the person of Christ. I shall show that Hick offers no compelling argument for giving up the traditional two-natures view of Chalcedon.

Six Christological claims

There are six separate claims that make up Hick's non-incarnational Christology. They are:

(1) Jesus did not teach that he himself was God Incarnate.
(2) The Chalcedonian two-natures doctrine of the person of Christ cannot be expressed in a religiously adequate fashion.

fact that senior British theologians and churchmen were claiming to hold to non-incarnational views of Christology. For some representative responses to the mythologists, see Michael Goulder (ed.), *Incarnation and Myth: The Debate Continued* (London: SCM Press, 1979); Brian Hebblethwaite, *The Incarnation*, passim; and John Coventry, 'The myth and the method', *Theology* 81 (1978), pp. 252–260. For an account of the development of non-incarnational Christology in nineteenth-century German liberal Protestantism, see Alister McGrath, *The Making of Modern German Christology, 1750–1990*, 2nd edn (Leicester: Apollos, 1994 [1987]), passim.

[3] Louisville: Westminster John Knox Press, 1993.
[4] For discussion of the development of Hick's Christology, see Gerald Loughlin, 'Squares and circles: John Hick and the doctrine of the Incarnation', in Harold Hewitt, Jr (ed.), *Problems in the Philosophy of Religion: Critical Studies of the Work of John Hick* (New York: St Martin's Press, 1991).

DIVINITY AND HUMANITY

(3) The historical and traditional two-natures doctrine has been used to justify great evils, such as wars, persecution, repression and genocide.

(4) The notion of Incarnation is better understood as a metaphor rather than as expressing some literal, metaphysical truth about the person of Christ.

(5) The life and teaching of Jesus challenge us to live a life pleasing to God. Jesus is the Lord who makes God real to Christians.

(6) This metaphorical understanding of the Incarnation fits with a doctrine of religious pluralism, whereby Christ's life and teaching are seen as one example of the religious life that can also be found, in different ways and forms, in other major world religions too. (This, for Hick, overcomes the tension between what he sees as Christological exclusivity and God's universal love for all.)[5]

We shall consider each of these claims in turn.

Did Jesus teach that he himself was God Incarnate?

First, on the question of whether or not Christ taught what was to become the classical doctrine of Incarnation, Hick is clear that 'the historical Jesus did not make the claim to deity that later Christian thought was to make for him: he did not understand himself to be God, or God the son, incarnate'.[6] Hick's argument for this relies upon a well-worn story about what can be known of the life and teaching of Christ, on the basis of historical-critical biblical scholarship. It seems to me that there is no single agreed version of this story or what it should contain. Some biblical scholars are far more sceptical about what can be known of the life of Christ than are others.[7]

---

[5] *The Metaphor of God Incarnate*, p. ix.   [6] Ibid., p. 27.

[7] Compare Harold Attridge: 'There remains enormous diversity among those who attempt to describe what Jesus really did, taught, and thought about himself. For some contemporary scholars he was a Hellenistic magician; for others, a Galilean charismatic

Nevertheless, the sort of story Hick wants to endorse is as follows: The only access we have to Jesus of Nazareth is through the documents of the New Testament and various apocryphal texts, like the Gospel of Thomas. These texts are the products (in the case of the canonical Gospels) of the early Christian communities, which had a vested interest in portraying Jesus as the Son of God. There is, therefore, a sharp distinction to be made between the Jesus of history, that is, the Jesus of the pre-Easter period, and the Christ of faith, that is, the person about whom the early church wrote, and whom they worshipped as the Son of God. It is very difficult to distinguish those sayings of the Jesus of history from those of the Christ of faith, because these sayings have been embedded in the canonical text of Scripture, which, in the case of the canonical Gospels, has gone through a complex process of assembly, editing and redaction. The final, canonical texts that we have reflect the different theologies of the ecclesial communities in which they were written. For instance, the Gospel of John is a far more theologically rich Christological statement than the Gospel of Mark, though both Gospels convey central ecclesiastical notions concerning the Christ of faith (though, perhaps not always the same notions). There is much controversy over the dating of the New Testament. But scholars tend to accept that the authors of the canonical Gospels were not present at the events they describe. In the case of John's Gospel (and perhaps some of the other Gospel accounts, depending on which New Testament scholars you believe), the theological sophistication of the Gospel points to a late date of completion, perhaps the end of the first century, or

or rabbi; for yet others, a prophetic reformer; for others, a sly teller of wry and engaging tales; for some he had grandiose ideas; for others, he eschewed them. In general the inquirer finds the Jesus that her historical method allows her to see.' 'Calling Jesus Christ', in Eleonore Stump and Thomas P. Flint (eds.), *Hermes and Athena* (Notre Dame: University of Notre Dame Press, 1993), p. 211. The story of the development of historical-critical scholarship has been set forth and criticized with admirable clarity by Roy A. Harrisville and Walter Sundberg, *The Bible in Modern Culture: Baruch Spinoza to Brevard Childs*, 2nd edn (Grand Rapids: Eerdmans, 2002 [1995]).

beginning of the second century, AD. In the case of Mark, usually thought to be the earliest extant Gospel, if we accept an early date of composition, say around AD 60, this is still about thirty years after the death of Jesus. So it seems that the Gospels are composed in a period of about a generation to two generations after the events they report took place, which is a considerable time after these things happened.

There is, therefore, only a very limited amount of material that we can know about the historical, pre-Easter, Jesus. Much of it is coloured by the presentation of the early Church communities who wrote the canonical Gospels. Nevertheless, it is extremely unlikely that Jesus ever indicated that he thought of himself as anything other than an itinerant Jewish rabbi, or a prophetic, perhaps messianic, figure. For a Jewish religious teacher of the period to claim to be divine, or to allude to this, would be tantamount to blasphemy. For the first-century Jewish mind, this would be unthinkable.

This has important implications for what we can know about Christ, and for whether Christ taught that he was a divine figure, either explicitly or by implication.[8] Given this historical-critical story,

---

[8] This is an important distinction in the historical-critical literature, and one that Hick picks up on. Most historical-critical scholars who are sceptical about what can be known of the life of Christ from the canonical Gospels are also dismissive of the idea that Christ made any explicit claim to divinity. Gospel material such as the 'I am' sayings of the Johannine texts is not usually thought to be genuine, but rather the words of the evangelist in the mouth of Christ. In the face of such criticisms of the textual evidence, scholars with a more expansive view of what can be known of the pre-Easter Jesus tend to opt for a weaker claim: Jesus implied his own divinity in things he did (forgiving sin, healing the sick, raising the dead, his attitude to observance of the Mosaic Law). Some take an even weaker view: Christ did not make either claim, but his disciples made it, in the light of the post-Easter events (resurrection appearances and ascension – however they are construed). My phrase 'either explicitly or by implication' is deliberately ambiguous. It seems to me that there is reason to believe that Christ made implicit claims to divinity. But he may have made explicit claims too. I do not think it a strong argument in favour of Christ's divinity to assert that, although he made no such claim about himself, his disciples did so because of what they saw and heard post-Easter. If, after my death, a group of my students began

it is very difficult to be sure of what Jesus believed about himself and his own mission. But, says Hick, although one cannot be certain on the basis of historical-critical scholarship alone that Jesus did not claim to be divine, an impressive range of historical-critical scholars have reached the conclusion that Jesus did not claim to be God Incarnate. Indeed, he cites an impressive range of theologians and biblical scholars who endorse a *Chalcedonian* Christology and yet maintain this very thing.[9]

But why should the theologian accept that Christ did not teach *anything* that can be construed as a claim to be divine, or as implying divinity? And if he did not make such a claim, why was it that the earliest Christians began to treat Christ as a divine figure, including him in the identity of the God of Israel, at a very early date in the development of Christian doctrine? We shall need to examine these two issues in turn. First, the question of why one should accept that Christ did not explicitly teach his own divinity, or else imply it. All the Chalcedonian Christologist needs in this instance is the idea that Christ made implicit claims to divinity. (There may be important reasons – discussed in some older historical-critical literature – why Christ would not have taught his own divinity explicitly, or at least, openly.[10]) In adjudicating the question of whether or not Jesus made an implicit claim to deity, Hick states:

> to claim that I had taught them repeatedly and emphatically that I was, in fact, Elvis Presley and would return to my ancestral home, that would probably not be taken as good evidence that I had made such claims, did think of myself as Elvis, or was Elvis.

[9] See *The Metaphor of God Incarnate*, pp. 27–28.

[10] I refer to the so-called 'messianic secret' of the Synoptic Gospels. There are indications in the first three Gospels that Christ tried to keep his identity a secret from the crowds and religious leaders because he feared that they would want to make him into a political messiah, or use his message for other, unpleasant, theological purposes. This messianic secret can be extended to include Christ's divinity too. An obvious claim to divinity would have meant certain death, as evidenced in John 8. It is consistent with this reading of Jesus' ministry that his utterances would have remained enigmatic, when he was faced with those in authority. Once again, this is what the Gospels demonstrate when Christ was before Pilate and Herod.

If one has already accepted a form of orthodox Christology one can reasonably interpret some of Jesus' words and actions, as presented by the Gospel writers, as implicitly supporting that belief. But it seems clear that one cannot justifiably arrive at the belief simply from the New Testament evidence as this has thus far been analysed and interpreted by the scholarly community.[11]

But this is a loaded statement, for two reasons. First, all that one requires, on the basis of Hick's claim here, is the *concept* of the God-Man, not the *belief* that there is a God-Man. An atheist could have the concept of the God-Man (by reading the Chalcedonian definition, say), and then read the canonical Gospels and find there the same concept in embryonic form, or find that Christ in the New Testament does make what appear to be implicit claims to divinity, consistent with the notion that Christ is the God-Man. But it does not follow from this that the atheist believes Christ to be the God-Man. One could certainly arrive at the conclusion that the New Testament documents teach that Christ is the God-Man *without forming the belief* that Christ is the God-Man. And I do not see why one could not also form the *belief* that Christ is the God-Man simply on the basis of the evidence of the New Testament documents. In fact, on the basis of anecdotal evidence, that is just what most people who profess to be Christians do claim. Hick seems to be confusing the concept involved with believing that concept to be true.

Secondly, what Hick wants us to believe is that there are two sorts of people: those who come to the Gospels with the eyes of faith, expecting to see there the Christ, the Son of God; and those who come to the text without any assumptions about whether or not Jesus of Nazareth was a divine figure, who simply let the evidence speak for itself, going where it leads. But this is a fiction. Historical-critical scholars whose methodological principles preclude the consideration of

---

[11] *The Metaphor of God Incarnate*, p. 33.

supernatural agency in history will *ex hypothesi* be sceptical about the possibility that certain sayings about Christ, or purporting to be from Christ, can be sayings of the historical Jesus. In fact, several recent studies of the methodology adopted by many historical-biblical critics have made this point.[12] All of which only confirms what George Tyrrell said nearly a century ago: 'The Christ that [Adolf von] Harnack [and, for our purposes, Hick] sees, looking back through nineteen centuries of Catholic darkness, is only the reflection of a Liberal Protestant face, seen at the bottom of a deep well.'[13] The Jesus of history that Hick believes can be found in the New Testament documents, and whose teaching does not include a claim (implicit or explicit) to divinity, is the reconstruction of contemporary scholars. But this reconstruction is also a revision of the Church's claims about Christ. Why should one trust the reconstruction of a group of scholars rather than the teaching of the Church down through the ages, the faith received and believed upon by the vast majority of Christians today? Why is this revisionist understanding of Christ's teaching in the canonical Gospels more reasonable or more reliable than the traditional one? The answer to this is not nearly as straightforward as it might at first appear, and is fraught with assumptions and presuppositions that are not always declared.[14]

Nor is it clear that a purely historical-critical approach to the canonical Gospel accounts of the life of Christ can be expected to

[12] See, for example, the essays collected together in Stump and Flint, *Hermes and Athena*; Alvin Plantinga, *Warranted Christian Belief* (New York: Oxford University Press, 2000), ch. 12; and Craig Bartholomew, C. Stephen Evans, Mary Healy and Murray Rae (eds.), *Behind the Text: History and Biblical Interpretation* (Carlisle: Paternoster Press, 2004).

[13] George Tyrrell, *Christianity at the Crossroads* (London: Longmans Green, 1909), p. 49.

[14] Space prevents a fuller explanation of this point. See, for instance, Plantinga's critique of what he calls Troeltschian and Duhemian types of historical-critical New Testament scholarship in *Warranted Christian Belief*, ch. 12. See also Richard Sturch, *The Word and the Christ: An Essay in Analytic Christology* (Oxford: Oxford University Press, 1991), Excursus 7, for a case study of this.

yield the *whole* truth about the historical Jesus. As Austin Farrer once observed, the historical method is like a net that is let down into the ocean in order to catch fish:

> No net will catch all the living matter in the water and no historical method will fish up the whole of live historical reality, unless we give to 'historical reality' the tautological sense of 'what our historical method fishes up'. There is plenty of history that will forever elude historical inquiry and it is pretty obvious that the supernatural being of Jesus Christ is some of that. The Christian faith is not believed on historical grounds alone, that is, on grounds which unaided history can establish: it is believed on living testimony of a special kind.[15]

In other words, if Jesus was God Incarnate as the Church has always believed, it does not necessarily follow that historical-critical methods could show that this was the case. Such historical-criticism may not be the right sort of tool for that kind of job. It is rather like measuring wind-speed using a Geiger counter. A Geiger counter is very good at measuring radiation levels in a particular area, but it cannot measure wind-speed because it is a device for measuring radiation levels – it is the wrong piece of equipment for that task.

At the very least, it is not clear that the fact that the canonical Gospels are the products of early Christian communities *entails* that these documents distort or exaggerate certain claims about Christ and his mission, in order to fit certain theological presuppositions these communities had about the person and work of Christ. Compare the words of another sort of textual critic, C. S. Lewis, on this subject. The belief that the meaning of the words of Jesus was quickly lost or distorted by his followers, only to be recovered by the tools of contemporary historical-critical scholarship, is comparable to the belief that the study of Plato was obscured or occluded

---

[15] Austin Farrer, *Interpretation and Belief* (London: SPCK, 1976), p. 127.

by scholars prior to his discovery by nineteenth-century idealists: 'One was brought up to believe that the real meaning of Plato had been misunderstood by Aristotle and widely travestied by the neo-Platonists, only to be recovered by the moderns. When recovered it turned out (most fortunately) that Plato had really been all along an English Hegelian, rather like T. H. Green.'[16] The reconstructed Jesus of contemporary historical-critical scholarship is not necessarily the historical Jesus recovered from the hands of those who would distort him. (He might be. But it is not *necessarily* the case that he is. That is, the historical-critical scholars who claim otherwise could be wrong.) Hick appears guilty of the genetic fallacy, which confuses questions of validity and logical order with questions of origin and temporal order.[17] It might be that the early Church had a vested interest in ensuring that the teaching of Christ was preserved largely intact.[18] If Christ were the Incarnate Word and made claims to that effect, then this would count as such a reason. So it is not obvious that the early Church's representation of Christ in the canonical Gospels is to be doubted *because* these Gospels are the work of the early Church. What the historical-critical scholar needs to show is that it is more likely than not, on the balance of evidence, that the early Church deliberately distorted the life and teaching of

---

[16] C. S. Lewis, 'Fern seed and elephants' in *Fern Seed and Elephants and Other Essays on Christianity*, ed. Walter Hooper (London: HarperCollins, 1975), p. 93.

[17] An example of this fallacy might be the following statement: 'The media claim that Senator Hurst was taking bribes. But we all know about the media's credibility, don't we?' The implication is that the media is inherently unreliable, so any claim it makes about whether or not Senator Hurst was taking bribes should be treated with scepticism. But it may be that this report is true. The fact that the media report it does not necessarily mean that it is a false report.

[18] I say 'largely intact' because it might be that certain peripheral matters were not preserved intact, such as the date and exact location of Christ's birth, or the place where he taught a certain parable, or the exact wording of what Christ said – after all, the canonical Gospels were written some time after the events they describe. Even if this were conceded to the historical-critical scholar, it does not follow from this that the Church deliberately distorted the substance of Christ's teaching.

the historical Jesus in the canonical Gospels. I am not claiming that historical-critical scholars must demonstrate beyond a reasonable doubt that the Church had a vested interest in distorting matters. Such a requirement would be too great for most historical scholarship. My point is merely that it is not obvious that the sceptical historical-critical conclusion about the life and teaching of Christ is the *only* reasonable reading of the data. It certainly does not seem to me that historical-critical scholarship has shown that it is most likely, on the balance of evidence, that the Church did distort the substance of Christ's teaching.

But aside from these problems with the argument from some historical-critical conclusions about the biblical data, there has recently been a move among New Testament scholars to reconsider received (that is, post-Enlightenment) scholarly wisdom about the self-understanding of Christ. Based on the fact that, very early in the history of the Church, Christ was included in the unique identity of the God of Israel, several leading New Testament scholars have begun to speak of an early high Christology as the only plausible explanation for the fact that the apostles and other leading members of the early Church treated Christ as a divine figure who was to be worshipped. Previously, it had been thought that early Christians regarded Jesus as a divine figure because late second-Temple Judaism admitted of a number of intermediary semi-divine figures, like angels, whose veneration had eroded the purity of traditional Jewish monotheism. However, scholars such as Richard Bauckham and Larry Hurtado have called this reading of late second-Temple Judaism into question. In the case of Bauckham, this is because he believes that late second-Temple Judaism had a concept of God, which, though robustly monotheistic, was flexible enough to include within it a notion of the divine Wisdom and the divine Word, which are identified with God, and applied to Christ. His 'surprising thesis' is that 'the highest possible Christology' was a part of the Christian Church 'even before any of the New Testament writings were written'. Furthermore:

The new Testament writers did not see their Jewish monotheistic heritage as in any way an obstacle to the inclusion of Jesus in the divine identity; they used its resources extensively in order precisely to include Jesus in the divine identity; and they saw in this inclusion of Jesus in the divine identity the fulfilment of the eschatological expectation of Jewish monotheism that the one God will be universally acknowledged as such in his universal rule over all things.[19]

This is not decisive evidence that Christ taught, either implicitly or explicitly, that he was divine, but it is a very important indication that his earliest disciples, who were Jewish monotheists, were proclaiming him to be someone included in the divine identity from the period between the death of Christ and the writing of the first Christian Scriptures. The most plausible explanation for this, according to the early-high-Christologists, is that the apostles believed that Christ was divine. It would be quite incredible to hold that these men, who had followed Jesus for the period of his public ministry, and had been appointed by him to serve as leaders of the new community he left behind, would so distort his teaching that they abandoned their strict Jewish monotheism for a form of Trinitarian theology within a matter of years after the death of Christ.

What this shows is that Hick's claim about the historical-critical consensus on the life of Christ – and what it is likely Christ that taught about himself – is questionable. It rests upon a certain historical-critical reading of the relevant Gospels which is not unimpeachable, and in any case, may not provide the right sort of tools for the theological claims Hick and others want to make. Moreover, the development of early high Christology casts quite a different light upon the development of the biblical material, and raises the real possibility that the highest possible Christology was part of the

---

[19] Richard Bauckham, *God Crucified: Monotheism and Christology in The New Testament* (Grand Rapids: Eerdmans, 1998), p. 27. See also Larry W. Hurtado, *One God, One Lord: Early Christian Devotion and Ancient Jewish Monotheism* (Philadelphia: Fortress Press, 1988), and J. D. G. Dunn, *Christology in the Making* (London: SCM Press, 1980).

Christian tradition from its very inception. (This last point also shows, incidentally, that Hick's claim to some received consensus among biblical scholars on these matters is not quite as secure as he seems to think it is.) All this means that Hick's assertion that Jesus did not teach that he was God Incarnate seems a lot less plausible than it might have appeared at first sight. It also provides a good argument for the contrary, and traditional, Christological claim that Christ implicitly taught that he himself was divine, because his first disciples began to treat him as part of the identity of the Jewish God from a very early period in the development of the Christian tradition.

The religious adequacy of the Chalcedonian two-natures doctrine

The second of Hick's claims was that the Chalcedonian two-natures doctrine cannot be expressed in a religiously adequate fashion. Earlier, in his time as one of the 'mythologizers' in *The Myth of God Incarnate* debate, Hick had taken the view that the two-natures doctrine was not just expressed in a religiously inadequate fashion, but was as logically contradictory as a square circle.[20] In his latest work, he has backed away from this strong claim.[21] This is sensible, not least because we cannot know *a priori* that the two-natures doctrine is incoherent without first establishing (a) exactly what the constituents of divinity and humanity consist in (or, perhaps better, what divinity and humanity do not consist in), and (b) that these constituents are mutually exclusive of one another. It is notoriously difficult to determine the necessary and sufficient conditions of being human, as we have already had cause to note earlier in this volume, even if the necessary and sufficient conditions of being divine are

[20] See Hick, *The Myth of God Incarnate*, p. 178.
[21] Notably *The Metaphor of God Incarnate*, ch. 5.

clearer because of revelation. Hence, Hick's initial claim was far too strong.[22]

Hick's recent view is, therefore, much weaker. What he says is that the Chalcedonian definition merely *asserts* that Christ is God Incarnate because of the hypostatic union. It does nothing to *explain* this paradox.[23] But, as was pointed out in the first chapter, appeals to mystery or to paradox should be distinguished from appeal to contradiction.[24]

A contradiction is derived from the conjunction of two mutually exclusive propositions, of the form '*p* and ~*p*'. If someone says, 'Jesus is only a man, and Jesus is not only a man', this would count as a contradiction, because such an utterance has the form '*p* and ~*p*'. However, if someone says, 'Jesus is fully human' and 'Jesus is not merely fully human', as Thomas Morris suggests we think of the two-natures doctrine, this is not a contradiction. Such an utterance has the form (*p* & *q*). If one person could be both fully human and also more than just human, then he would be fully but not merely human as other human beings are.[25] How can Christ be both fully and not merely human? The Chalcedonian answer is that he has two natures in hypostatic union. But what does this mean, exactly? That Christ is one person who somehow has a fully human and a fully divine nature subsisting together in his person for the duration

---

[22] This point has been made by Thomas Morris and others. Sarah Coakley has reiterated it in 'What Does Chalcedon Solve and What Does it Not? Some Reflections on the Status and Meaning of the Chalcedonian "Definition"' in Stephen Davis, Daniel Kendall and Gerald O'Collins (eds.), *The Incarnation* (Oxford: Oxford University Press, 2002).

[23] *The Metaphor of God Incarnate*, p. 48. Gavin D'Costa pointed out to me that this weaker view appears in earlier writings of Hick alongside the stronger. In his latest work, the stronger claim drops out.

[24] Compare Stephen Davis, 'John Hick on Incarnation and Trinity', in Stephen Davis, Brian Kendall and Gerald O'Collins (eds.), *The Trinity* (Oxford: Oxford University Press, 1999), pp. 257ff.

[25] This is the case independently of whether or not one adopts Morris's two-minds Christology.

of Incarnation. Beyond this lies mystery. Hick thinks that beyond this lies paradox. In either case, this need not be a problem for the Chalcedonian theologian. A mystery is some problem beyond the grasp of reason. But this need not mean that mysteries are thinly veiled contradictions. Much classical Christian doctrine appeals to mystery. How can God be three persons in one being? How can Christ be the God-Man? Such things may *appear* contradictory, but, given that they are revealed truths, one has good reason to believe them to be true. The point about such appeals to mystery, and why they are not simply irresponsible get-outs, is that (a) it is possible to locate the area of mystery precisely and (b) it is possible to say precisely in what the mystery consists. Furthermore, it is plausible to suppose that there will be mystery in *sui generis* divine–human relations such as is found in the doctrine of the Incarnation. It is one thing to say that there is no adequate explanation of the two-natures doctrine of Chalcedon that has been given in the Christian tradition. It is quite another to claim that there can be no such explanation.

Sarah Coakley is one contemporary representative of the view that the Chalcedonian definition is rather like a fence or boundary around the mystery of Incarnation. What it does is establish what cannot be said of Christ, consistent with taking seriously the full range of New Testament data about him and denying certain Christological heresies, such as Apollinarianism and Nestorianism. There is also a sense in which the Chalcedonian settlement is a piece of apophatic, or negative, theology: it states what the two-natures doctrine is not. It also deploys certain technical, metaphysical notions to make some things about this union clear. However, it does not attempt to make plain what is mysterious, nor could it begin to do so, because the precise nature of the Incarnation is not revealed in Scripture. And, since the Incarnation, like the Trinity, is a revealed doctrine, it is sufficient for the purposes of Christian belief that the Christian hold to what has been revealed, even though (some of) the content of that revelation is mysterious. The Christian is not thereby committed to one or other metaphysical theory of how exactly the two natures subsist in the hypostatic union beyond what has been revealed and what the Church has ratified in the catholic creeds, including Chalcedon.

All this is to say that Hick's criticism that there has, to date, been no entirely satisfactory account of the two-natures doctrine is only to be expected if this is a divine mystery. The fact that the Incarnation has been universally understood in the Christian Church as a divine mystery does not entail that it is therefore a contradiction. It may entail certain paradoxes, meaning, here, certain notions that are unexpected or peculiar. But it does not entail paradox if, as Hick has done in the past, one takes this to mean a species of contradiction.[26]

Finally, and merely *ad hominem*, Hick accepts paradoxes without further explanation in two areas of his own thinking. In his Christology, he happily embraces a version of Donald Baillie's celebrated paradox of grace. And in his religious pluralism (about which, more anon), he is willing to accept as true both Christian teaching that there is a personal God and the Vedantic Hindu concept that 'God' is an impersonal force. They are both phenomenal truths about some noumenal reality – the Real – that is beyond the grasp of any one religious tradition. Whatever else one makes of this, it looks paradoxical, perhaps contradictory. It seems paradoxical to say that the Real is both a personal being and an impersonal force. This is not just a problem of epistemic vantage (I can see this one aspect of the Real that seems slightly different from where you are standing, rather as a building appears to have a rectangular side when viewed from one angle, but a rhomboidal side when viewed from another angle). It is a problem of conflicting metaphysical claims about the nature of God/the Real. Hick seems to want to say that these two claims are just about epistemic vantage. For the Hindu, 'God' is impersonal; for the Christian, he is personal. But, according to Hick, these are two

---

[26] It seems to me that Hick is right to say there is technically no satisfactory account of the two-natures doctrine, but wrong to think that this is because the doctrine is unintelligible. It may be possible to give an adequate account of the two-natures doctrine, provided it is borne in mind that any such account would not be able to offer a complete explanation of the doctrine, due to its being a divine mystery.

different appearances of one noumenal reality. The problem with this is that these two predicates, 'personal being' and 'impersonal force', do not appear to be compatible with one another. Nor, according to the Christian, is it the case that the predicate 'personal being' is merely an appearance of some noumenal reality beyond his or her grasp.

It is, to say the least, curious that Hick is most happy with paradox or mystery when it comes to the explanation of his own religious pluralism, but unwilling to tolerate it in traditional Christology.[27]

The great evils perpetrated for the sake of the two-natures doctrine

This particular criticism is extremely tenuous. It relies upon there being some clear and established relation between a two-natures doctrine of the Incarnation and certain atrocities or evils that have been perpetrated. Hick says:

> These evils – anti-Semitism; the colonial exploitation of the Third (or two thirds) World; Western patriarchalism; and the Christian superiority-complex in relation to the peoples of other faiths – have not been caused by the incarnation dogma . . . But [we are] concerned, not with the fact of these evils as such but with the ways in which they have been defended by appeal to the idea of Jesus' deity. The conclusion is not that the doctrine is thereby shown to be false, but a recognition that it is inherently liable to dangerous misuse by fallen human nature.[28]

But the fact that something is liable to misuse does not mean that it should not be used properly. A little salt on one's meal is not likely to

---

[27] A similar point is made by Davis, 'John Hick on the Incarnation and Trinity'. Hick does attend to this issue, albeit inadequately, in *An Interpretation of Religion: Human Responses to the Transcendent* (London: Macmillan, 1989), ch. 14.

[28] *The Metaphor of God Incarnate*, p. 80.

cause any damage, and may add flavour to the meat. But too much salt in one's diet may be a contributing factor to congestive heart failure. The same applies to any number of things, apart from the two-natures doctrine of the Incarnation, that have a proper use and are capable of being misused. Take the claim, 'All men are born equal.' As George Orwell showed in *Animal Farm*, even such an important moral notion as this can be misused. (Recall the way in which Napoleon and the other pigs subvert the dictum 'All animals are equal' by adding, '*but some animals are more equal than others*'.) The fact that the two-natures doctrine has been used as a justification for various crimes down the centuries, from crusading to racial hatred, shows only that this doctrine, like so many other religious doctrines, has been used as the nominal justification for all sorts of human wickedness. It says absolutely nothing about the truth or falsity of the doctrine itself. This Hickian claim is a deliberate attempt to apply a sort of 'guilt by association' to the two-natures doctrine. But as a criticism of the truth of the doctrine it is entirely beside the point.[29]

Incarnation, metaphor and the life and teaching of Christ

We shall consider the fourth and fifth claims together. As we have already seen, Hick is clear that his Christology is not a way of reading the Chalcedonian definition, but a replacement for it. He says that 'a Chalcedonian-type Christology cannot be spelt out as a literal theory in any religiously acceptable way'.[30] The alternative to this that is most

---

[29] In response to this sort of criticism by Hick, it is tempting to point out the fact that a number of theologically liberal Christian thinkers have, in the past, endorsed political regimes or wars that are just as despicable as those Hick points to with regard to Chalcedonian Christology. One thinks of Karl Barth's disgust on finding that almost all his former theological teachers had signed a declaration in support of Kaiser Wilhelm II at the beginning of the First World War. See MacGrath, *The Making of Modern German Christology*, ch. 6.

[30] *The Metaphor of God Incarnate*, p. 104.

appealing, according to Hick, is to think of the Incarnation as a sort of extended metaphor, or myth:

> Metaphor can readily develop into myth in the sense of a powerful complex of ideas, usually in story form, which is not literally true but which may nevertheless be true in the practical sense that it tends to evoke an appropriate dispositional attitude to its subject matter. A myth, so defined, is a much extended metaphor.

He applies this understanding of metaphor as extended myth to the Incarnation as follows:

> The myth of God incarnate is the story of the pre-existent divine Son descending into human life, dying to atone for the sins of the world, thereby revealing the divine nature, and returning into the eternal life of the Trinity. The mythic story expresses the significance of a point in history where we can see human life lived in faithful response to God and see God's nature reflected in that human response.[31]

But what does Hick mean by this usage of 'myth' and 'metaphor' in this interchangeable fashion? He contrasts the literal meaning of a word, which is, roughly speaking, its dictionary definition, with a metaphorical meaning. The use of metaphor presupposes a departure from a dictionary definition. Although the precise sense in which metaphor differs from a dictionary-defined word is difficult to make clear, there is a central notion of the transference of meaning from one word to another, via an association or relation between the two words through usage, as in phrases like 'Rock of Ages', 'Ancient of Days' or 'Lamb of God' as applied to God or Christ. This gives rise to a range of meanings that can be attached to a metaphor:

> A metaphor's central thrust can be literally translated, but its ramifying overtones and emotional colour are variable and changing and thus are not translatable without remainder into a definitive list of

---

[31] Ibid., pp. 105–106.

literal propositions. The use of metaphor is accordingly a different kind of speech-act from the listing of identifiable similarities. Metaphorical speech is indeed akin to poetry, and shares its non-translatability into literal prose.[32]

Let us grant that a metaphor involves the transference of meaning from one word to another in some associative relation, as Hick maintains is the case. (The notion of something that is ancient, and full of days – an old man, say, or some object that has been around since time immemorial – becomes associated with the concept of the God of Israel, one who is eternal, or everlasting. The result is the metaphorical ascription to God of the title 'Ancient of Days'.) It cannot be translated into some literal word, meaning, according to Hick, a word that can be defined by its dictionary definition. The very transference-relation involved in uttering or writing a metaphor admits of a number of different possible meanings for that metaphor. There is, therefore, a built-in ambiguity to the notion of metaphor, as Hick understands it. This ambiguity has to do with the range of meaning a given metaphor may have. He has also said that a myth is an elaborate, or rich, metaphor. It tells us a story that is non-literal. It is not possible to translate a myth into some comprehensive literal, propositional truth, which has no remainder. So a myth, like a piece of epic poetry, tells us a story, which 'tends to evoke an appropriate dispositional attitude to its subject matter'.

But it seems to do more than that for Hick. It also conveys certain propositional truths, such as 'This story is not to be understood as literally true', or 'This story has the following non-literal interpretation (among other, potential interpretations)', and so on. That is, it is not the case that myths, as Hick describes them, convey *no* propositional content, but instead merely evoke an appropriate dispositional attitude to the subject matter. A myth may do that, but it does more than that because it conveys certain propositions about the content of the myth, like the fact that a mythical story is not to be understood in a literal way. We can account for this by saying that a myth conveys certain general propositions about the non-literal nature of the content of the mythic story that are common to all myths, and some propositions about the nature of this particular myth ('This myth about Theseus and the Minotaur is to be taken non-literally', 'This myth expresses the moral truth *x*', and so on). But the myth itself does not express a single propositional truth that exhausts the content of the myth. Instead, it elicits a certain attitude, as does poetry. Thus, for instance, C. S. Lewis in his discussion of myth says:

> The first hearing [of a myth] is chiefly valuable in introducing us to a permanent object of contemplation . . . which works upon us by its peculiar flavour or quality, rather as a smell or a chord does . . . The experience is not only grave but awe-inspiring. We feel it to be numinous. It is as if something of great moment had been communicated to us. The recurrent efforts of the mind to grasp – we mean, chiefly, to conceptualise – this something, are seen in the persistent tendency of humanity to provide myths with allegorical explanations. And after all allegories have been tried, the myth itself continues to feel more important than they.[33]

There is something of this in Hick's account. But he wants to say that the myth of God Incarnate also conveys certain propositions about the Incarnation. In particular, it shows that this story is not literally about the God-Man.

It is curious that Hick thinks metaphor should be used *in place of* literal, realist language about the Incarnation. It by no means follows from the fact that metaphor is deployed for a particular theological purpose that the truth conveyed should be non-literal. If I were to say to my child, 'Do not imbibe alcoholic drinks; they are brewed in the bowels of Beelzebub', he would understand the metaphor to

---

[33] C. S. Lewis, *An Experiment in Criticism* (Cambridge: Cambridge University Press, 1961), pp. 43–44, cited in Sturch, *The Word and the Christ*, p. 238.

convey, among other things, the realist claim that drinking alcohol is bad for you. It would be perverse to construe this metaphor as conveying, 'It has often been thought that alcohol was brewed by Lucifer in his own alimentary canal, and then deposited in casks at the brewers. But this is just a myth.' Or, 'It has often been thought that alcohol is bad for you, but this is not to be taken literally.' Yet Hick maintains that metaphorical language, when used of the Incarnation, entails a sort of demythologizing programme. That is, it involves stripping away realist language of a literal Incarnation, to be replaced by a non-literal picture of the way in which Christ reveals something of God in his life and teaching. But this seems too strong, and is not warranted on the basis of the characterization of metaphor he offers. It might have been better had Hick abandoned the project of translating Chalcedonian language into the language of metaphor, and admitted from the beginning that his own account is simply a non-incarnational Christology, *sans* metaphorical paraphernalia.[34]

Nevertheless, what Hick proposes in place of traditional incarnational Christology is an understanding of Christ as a model religious teacher, who, like other major religious teachers, gives us important moral principles and the moral example of his life. On this way of thinking, Christ is just one of a number of such religious teachers, including Gautama Buddha, Muhammad and the Sikh Gurus. He is not the only supreme moral example, or the religious teacher whose intimacy with God surpasses that of other, similar religious teachers. In this respect, Hick refuses to absolutize Christ's person and work.[35]

Some theologians, like Donald Baillie or Geoffrey Lampe – both cited by Hick in his work – have tried to maintain a non-incarnational

---

[34] A similar point about the language of myth and metaphor in this Incarnation is made by Richard Sturch in *The Word and The Christ*, Excursus 1.

[35] See, e.g., John Hick, *Disputed Questions in Theology and Philosophy of Religion* (New Haven: Yale University Press, 1993), ch. 5.

or 'inspiration' Christology, while retaining the supreme significance of Christ as moral exemplar.[36] But, as Hick points out, once one has given up the notion of Incarnation, there is no reason to retain the idea that Christ's life, death and resurrection are unique, or that Christ's access to God is unsurpassable. Such issues are not essential components of non-incarnational Christologies. For, according to such Christologies, Christ's life becomes one among a number of lives which have crucial religious significance for different religious traditions. Those who, like Donald Baillie or Geoffrey Lampe, retain a version of inspiration Christology will no doubt demur from this. But if the way in which Christ was 'inspired' is just a greater degree of inspiration than is enjoyed by most other human beings, then it is difficult to see how one could claim that it is impossible for anyone else to be inspired in a similar fashion. We might say that the works of Michelangelo Merisi da Caravaggio bear the marks of a greater degree of artistic inspiration than the *Far Side* cartoons of Gary Larson. But the difference, like the difference assumed by inspiration and Spirit Christologies, is one of degree, not of kind. It is not impossible to conceive of an artist whose works bear the marks of the same degree of inspiration as Caravaggio's works, a degree of inspiration that sets them apart as a master of their craft. One example might be Rembrandt van Rijn, another, Lucian Freud. In a similar way, claims Hick, there are other spiritual masters

---

[36] Hick speaks of 'inspiration Christology' and, in the case of Lampe, a 'Spirit Christology'. For our purposes, an inspiration Christology is one that denies the Incarnation but retains the notion that Christ offers a moral example and set of teachings, which have shaped, and continue to shape, the lives of Christians. A Spirit Christology might be a version of inspiration Christology, if 'Spirit Christology' means that Christ was inspired, or enabled by the Holy Spirit, to live a life of supreme God-consciousness. But 'Spirit Christology' could mean something more robust than this. For instance, if someone claimed that the Incarnation consisted in the third person of the Trinity taking on human flesh, this might be a Spirit Christology in a rather idiosyncratic sense of that term. But this is not Lampe's view, and it is not clear to me that Lampe's Christology is really much more than a 'Spirit Christology' in the first, weaker, sense of the term.

apart from Christ, whose work is venerated in different religious traditions.

On a Chalcedonian view, although it might be that the Word is in a perichoretic relation with Christ's humanity that is more intimate by degree than the way in which he penetrates any other creature, the crucial difference is that there is an *Incarnation* involved. Christ is the God-Man. The property 'being God Incarnate' does not admit of degrees. If an object has this property, it cannot have more of this property. We might say it is a non-scaling property. It is not the case that one object could have the property 'being God Incarnate' and another the property 'being more God Incarnate' or 'being God Incarnate maximally'. Either an object has this property and is God Incarnate, or it does not and is not. The same cannot be said for an inspiration Christology that is non-incarnational. The property 'being inspired by God' is a scaling property. Some human beings are recipients of greater divine inspiration than others and, plausibly, a number of human beings are recipients of an order of divine inspiration that sets them apart from other human beings as great religious teachers, like Jesus, Gautama or Muhammad. Perhaps this scaling property has a threshold beyond which there are only religious teachers of a similar moral excellence, rather as one might think that a person can have more or less nobility, but not more nobility that a queen or a king (if one is a king or queen, one is as noble as other princes). But even if this is true, there could be more than one such religious teacher, just as there are different monarchs in different kingdoms. There still seems to be no good reason to think that Christ's moral example, or teaching, is of a different *order* from other paradigmatic religious teachers.[37]

37 This should not be taken to imply that there could not be more than one Incarnation. There is not space to deal with this in detail here, but even if there were two persons who were God Incarnate, the relation between such persons would be of a logically different order from that between two other persons who were merely particularly 'inspired' by God. So, my point is not about the uniqueness of Christ in the numerical sense. It is about the fact that 'being God Incarnate' is the property that sets Christ

So, on Hick's Christological programme, the Incarnation needs to be demythologized. Christ is said to 'incarnate' God only in the following sorts of ways: as Christ did the will of God, God worked through him and Christ 'incarnated' God; in so doing, Christ modelled the sort of life we should live, 'incarnating' the way in which God wants us to live; and as Christ's life demonstrated the love of God in his self-giving to others, he 'incarnated' God's love.[38]

Christology and religious pluralism

Hick's Christology is part of his wider programme of the advocacy of religious pluralism, as the title of his monograph makes clear.[39] But there seems to be a tension between his expressed views about God and Christology on the one hand, and his views on religious pluralism on the other. In dealing with Christology, Hick is willing to adopt the language of classical theism. Such language is irreducibly realist in a strong sense. That is, classical theistic language is language about some putative entity, God. Such language corresponds to a real entity about which we can know certain propositions, because religious language has cognitive content. But, although elsewhere (e.g. in his *An Interpretation of Religion*) Hick retains his theological realism,

apart from other human beings who are merely human. If one refuses to entertain the notion that Christ has this property, then one removes one important reason for insisting that Christ is unique among other human beings.

[38] *The Metaphor of God Incarnate*, p. 105.

[39] There is a considerable literature on Hick's religious pluralism. The reader is directed to several representative treatments of this. Philosophical treatments include the feschrift for William Alston: Thomas D. Senor (ed.), *The Rationality of Belief and the Plurality of Faith: Essays in Honor of William P. Alston* (Ithaca: Cornell University Press, 1995) – see the essays by Alvin Plantinga and Peter van Inwagen in particular. In addition, *Faith and Philosophy* 14/3 (1997) includes a symposium on this topic. Theological treatments of Hick's pluralism include Gavin D'Costa, *John Hick's Theology of Religions: A Critical Evaluation* (Lanham: Rowman and Littlefield, 1988), and Christopher Sinkinson, *The Universe of Faiths: A Critical Study of John Hick's Religious Pluralism* (Carlisle: Paternoster Press, 2001).

he rejects the language of classical theism. In fact, Hick claims that, if religious pluralism is true, theological language about God that refers to the Deity as a personal being is only phenomenal language about how things truly appear, but not about how they truly are. There is no God, as such. Instead, there is the Real, which is some noumenal reality beyond the phenomenal religious language that is used to describe God in the theistic religions, and also beyond the conceptions of a religious ultimate or a ground of being assumed in non-theistic religions such as Vedantic Hinduism or Theravada Buddhism. This Real is neither personal nor impersonal, according to Hick, because the Real is a reality beyond our conceptualizing of him/her/it:

> We cannot apply to the Real *an sich* the characteristics encountered in its *personae* and *impersonae*. Thus it cannot be said to be one or many, person or thing, conscious or unconscious, purposive or non-purposive, substance or process, good or evil, loving or hating. None of the descriptive terms that apply within the realm of human experience can apply literally to the unexperienceable reality that underlies that realm. All that we can say is that we postulate the Real *an sich* as the ultimate ground of the intentional objects of the different forms of religious thought-and-experience.[40]

Aside from the fact that this is self-contradictory[41] (a condition which is usually thought to be fatal to any argument), such a view of the Real is a far cry from a theistic conception of God, let alone the God and Father of our Lord Jesus Christ. If this Real is neither personal nor impersonal, and if all religious language about this entity (assuming that one can refer to the Real as an entity in some univocal

---

[40] Hick, *An Interpretation of Religion*, p. 350.

[41] It is self-contradictory because Hick claims (a) that the Real is beyond all conceptualizing of it and (b) that he knows that the Real is beyond all conceptualizing of it. But then, he must be able to know at least two things about the Real that are conceptual, namely (a) and (b). However, clearly he cannot know these two things if the Real is beyond all conceptualizing of it.

fashion) is, strictly speaking, false because she/he/it is beyond all conceptions of who she/he/it is, then two important theological consequences follow from this. First, Christian theological language, including language about the Incarnation, turns out to be untruthful. However, sometimes Hick says that although such language does not adequately express the Real, it is proximate, or analogous, or metaphorical language about the Real, about which, on Hick's view, nothing certain can be known in anything other than a phenomenal fashion. (Of course, according to Hick we can be certain that nothing certain is known of the nature of this entity, but that is another matter.)

Second, and following on from this, it is very difficult to see how Hick can be so sure that Christ is not the supreme or unique representative of such an entity. For, by his own admission, Hick, like the rest of us, is actually ignorant of the nature of the Real. For all he knows, Christ *is* the ultimate and unique revelation of the Real to human beings, accommodated to the limitations of human understanding about the Real. (For that matter, perhaps Gautama Buddha is the one religious teacher whose teaching is the most adequate conception of the Real. My point is that one of the religious traditions Hick counts as within the orbit of his religious pluralism could be religiously ultimate, for all we know.) Of course, Hick could deny this, but on what grounds?[42] Not on the grounds of his own particular brand of religious pluralism, because he has already conceded that he cannot know – no mere human being can know – the nature of the Real. So it is possible, for all we know, and given the structure of Hick's religious agnosticism about the nature of the Real, that the

---

[42] I suppose Hick could allow that one of the religious traditions he discusses could be ultimate, but that this is less likely than his own pluralistic hypothesis, according to which no one religious tradition has greater access to the metaphysical truth of the matter than another. But in fact he claims that no one religious tradition can have greater epistemic access to the metaphysical truth of the matter. See *An Interpretation of Religion*, ch. 13.

Real really has revealed something of herself/himself/itself in some ultimate if partial and limited way, in the person and work of Christ.

Hick's religious pluralism, as it bears upon his Christology, is ambiguous. It could be taken to mean that all talk of Incarnation, metaphorical or literal, is strictly speaking false, because such language has no purchase in the noumenal reality of the Real. Or, it could be that Christian religious language is proximately true, or analogously true, to something in the nature of the Real. It could also be that the Christian religion is unique in this respect, and that there is a sense in which the doctrinal content of Christianity reveals more of the Real than any other religious tradition. In which case, different religious traditions do not have epistemic parity when it comes to the metaphysical truth of the matter. Hick denies this last claim, but for no good reason, given the structure of his own pluralistic hypothesis.

Two more problems with Hick's Christology

There are two final points to make, one of which merely highlights the problem incarnational Christologists have with Hick's account, the other of which points out the religious inadequacy of Hick's Christology.

As we have seen in the foregoing, much of the force of Hick's account depends upon intuitions about the divine nature that conflict with those intuitions rooted in traditional, Chalcedonian-incarnational accounts of Christology.[43] To the extent the intuitions that inform his argument are shared by his readers, Hick's Christology will have some currency. But for those whose theological

---

43 One could have an account of Christology that was incarnational but not Chalcedonian, such as Nestorianism, monophysitism or modalism. But, for the sake of the argument and in keeping with the rest of this book, I shall assume in what follows that the incarnational Christology we are interested in is Chalcedonian.

proclivities favour a doctrine of Incarnation, Hick's intuitions will have little or no force whatsoever. Much depends on the intuitions that inform one's reasoning. For Hick, it is intuitions like 'God is not a being who is capable of becoming incarnate', or 'Only a Christology hospitable to religious pluralism can be true', that inform the arguments he offers. But no defender of Chalcedonian Christology will find such intuitions plausible. Hence, Chalcedonian Christologists and non-incarnational Christologists like Hick inevitably reach a conceptual impasse.

This brings us to a second and related point. Hick's Christology is religiously inadequate from the point of view of Christian theology. There is nothing in what Hick says that a simple theist could not affirm.[44] By a 'simple theist', I mean someone who holds to the tenets of theism without any specifically Christian theological claims such as the Trinity or Incarnation. Such a person could affirm without cavil all that Hick says about the person and work of Christ. A simple theist could endorse the view that Christ is a moral example whose life and teaching is a model for other human beings to imitate. Such a person could also affirm that Christ was one great religious teacher among a number of such religiously significant individuals. The simple theist could also affirm that Christ was an agent of God on earth, that he embodied certain important moral ideals and that Christians are reasonable to seek to follow Christ as their lord (taken, as Stephen Davis points out, as a guru, or teacher, which is what Hick's Christ amounts to[45]). Even Hick's religious pluralism is no obstacle for the simple theist. Such a person could affirm all the constituents of Hick's neo-Kantian approach to the Real, including the denial of the noumenal truth of the Trinity that belongs with

---

[44] In fact, as Gavin D'Costa pointed out to me, there is nothing in Hick's pluralist hypothesis that an agnostic could not affirm! I leave it to the reader to make the relevant adjustments to the following criticism of Hick in order to run an 'agnostic' version of the objection.

[45] Davis makes this point in several places. See, for instance, 'John Hick on Incarnation and Trinity', pp. 266–267.

his religious pluralism. (The Trinity, like the Incarnation, is at best a metaphor or picture of something that is beyond all phenomenal representation or expression, because the Real is beyond all phenomenal representation or expression.[46]) All of which should give the Christian theologian pause for thought. If the central and defining tenets of Hick's Christology may all be affirmed without holding to any distinctively Christian doctrine, then Hick's Christology seems religiously inadequate from the standpoint of Christian theism.

It is not that, taken from a Chalcedonian point of view, the central notions of Christ as moral exemplar or great religious teacher are false. It is rather that they are insufficient for a complete account of Christology. If Christ is *merely* a moral example in his life and work, or if he is *merely* one among several great religious teachers, then some important – indeed, crucial – features of the Christian account of the person and work of Christ are conspicuously absent. A Christology that fails to give an adequate account of these other features – features expressed in incarnational Christology – fails to give an account of Christ that is satisfactory, from the point of view of Christian theology. It is rather like giving an account of Shakespeare that leaves out the fact that he wrote some of the finest tragedies, comedies and sonnets ever penned by human hand. Such an account of Shakespeare would not necessarily be false, provided the information that *was* supplied about him was true. But it would be totally inadequate as an account of who he was and his importance for subsequent generations of English-speaking people.

This will not worry Hick unduly. His Christology is, after all, explicitly pluralist in its religious orientation. Once one has conceded that the traditional Christological claims inextricably bound up with a doctrine of Incarnation need to be excised in order for the doctrine to be of contemporary use, one has given up what is at the heart of the Christian claim about Christ. On the basis of Hick's religious pluralism, it would seem that the fact that his Christology can be

---

[46] See Davis, ibid., pp. 268ff., for a treatment of Hick on the Trinity.

affirmed in all its details by a simple theist is a virtue, not a vice. But this hardly recommends it to those who wish to retain a Chalcedonian Christology.

Conclusions

The fact that someone who was not a Christian could affirm Hick's Christology *in toto* seems to me to raise very serious questions about whether it can be called a Christian account of the person of Christ at all. There are other reasons for thinking that Hick's Christology is not a viable alternative to an incarnational account. I have shown how each of the claims that make up Hick's argument can be challenged. I have also shown that there are elements of Hick's argument that are unsatisfactory, even beside the point. Where it has been to the point, Hick's argument is less than convincing. He has certainly not shown that incarnational Christology is religiously inadequate. What he has demonstrated is that one account of non-incarnational Christology, his own account, is not religiously adequate for Christian theology. Hick's view is an interesting piece of speculation about how one understanding of the person of Christ could be compatible with a certain construal of the question of religious diversity. But it holds no terror for the Christian committed to incarnational Christology, for whom it is either a diverting but false report of who Christ is, or a dangerous heresy that should be resisted.

Index